T0311536

LATINO COMMUNITIES

EMERGING VOICES
POLITICAL, SOCIAL, CULTURAL, AND LEGAL ISSUES

edited by

ANTOINETTE SEDILLO LOPEZ
UNIVERSITY OF NEW MEXICO

A ROUTLEDGE SERIES

Colegio Cesar Chavez poster by Daniel Desiga.

COLEGIO CESAR CHAVEZ, 1973–1983

A Chicano Struggle for Educational Self-Determination

CARLOS S. MALDONADO

Routledge
Taylor & Francis Group

NEW YORK AND LONDON

Published in 2000 by
Routledge
711 Third Avenue, New York, NY 10017
2 Park Square, Milton Park, Abingdon, Oxfordshire OX14 4RN

First issued in paperback 2016

Routledge is an imprint of the Taylor and Francis Group, an informa business

Library of Congress Cataloging-in-Publication Data
Maldonado, Carlos S.
    Colegio Cesar Chavez, 1973–1983 : a Chicano struggle for educational self-determination / Carlos S. Maldonado.
        p. cm. — (Latino communities)
    Includes bibliographical references (p.) and index.
    ISBN 0-8153-3631-4 (alk. paper)
    1. Colegio Cesar Chavez (Mount Angel, Or.)—History. 2. Hispanic Americans—Education (Higher)—Oregon. I. Title. II. Series.
LD1061.C79 2000
378.795'37—dc21   00-027245

ISBN 13: 978-1-138-97103-5 (pbk)
ISBN 13: 978-0-8153-3631-0 (hbk)

Publisher's Note
The publisher has gone to great lengths to ensure the quality of this reprint but points out that some imperfections in the original may be apparent.

Dedication

Para mi amiga y esposa, Rachel Leona Maldonado y en memoria de mi madre, Herminia Saldivar Monjaras 1928–1988.

Contents

Figures

Illustrations

Preface

Historian Laurence Veysey argued that diversity is a unique characteristic of American higher education. This diversity has been premised on the varied viewpoints of historical leaders in American higher education.[1] According to the U.S Department of Education's 1997 Directory of Postsecondary Institutions, there are 9,837 postsecondary institutions in the U.S. Of these, 4,457 institutions are degree granting.[2] These institutions represent a diverse collection of institutions. They include public and private schools; 2 vs 4 year schools; Black and tribal colleges; women's colleges; church founded and operated colleges; corporate/industry schools; liberal arts, research, and teaching colleges; a few experimental colleges; and others. The Carnegie Foundation issued a periodic report titled: "A Classification of Institutions of Higher Education" to help bring more categorical or definitional precision in researching higher education and higher educational institutions. Their most recent edition, 1987, affirms the notion that institutional diversity in higher educational institutions is alive and well.[3] In general terms, I agree with this conclusion. Yet, I would argue that America's educational institutional diversity has certainly suffered with the closing of Chicano colleges founded in the 1970s.

Historically, ethnic higher educational institutions (Black, tribal and Chicano colleges) as noted, have been part of this diversity. Yet, historical investigations of minority institutions have been sparse and inadequate. This is particularly true of Chicano colleges founded during the early 1970s. To understand and appreciate America's higher educational diversity, it is necessary to become aware of and understand the role of minority higher educational institutions including

Chicano colleges. It is disappointing to note that as of 1999, there exists marginal research focusing on Chicano educational initiatives which emerged in the 1970s. The need for researching Chicano educational initiatives has become more urgent since all Chicano colleges founded during this period have closed their doors. This study provides an institutional history of Colegio Cesar Chavez, founded in Mt. Angel, Oregon. It serves to document a fragment of Chicano educational history and acquaint the reader with this history. Likewise, this study provides a glimpse into the link between Colegio and the Chicano community in the Pacific Northwest.

This study on Colegio Cesar Chavez is also important in underscoring the continuing educational marginality impacting Chicanos in K-12 and higher education. Soon we will enter the 21st century. The poor participation levels of Chicanos in postsecondary education, which Chicano colleges addressed 25–30 years ago, still remains a significant issue. Eventhough more Chicanos aged 18–24 are enrolling in college in the 1990s, as of 1996 Chicano high school graduates still lag nine percentage points behind whites in the same age group. Enrollment in college by Chicano high school graduates in the age cohorts of 25–34 and 35 or older, has in fact declined between 1976 and 1996. College completion and graduate education likewise continues to be a significant issue for Chicanos.[4] The recent publication, *The Elusive Quest for Equality: 150 Years of Chicana/Chicano Education* (1999) highlights the history and status of Chicano education.[5] The book's title reaffirms the notion that educational opportunity and equity for Chicanos continues to be an unmet goal.

While access to mainstream higher educational institutions should be pursued by Chicanos, the issue of choice should likewise be an important consideration. This study provides a foundation for future studies investigating the need and feasibility of Chicano colleges in expanding institutional choice and institutional diversity in American higher education. The interest in Chicano educational initiatives is ongoing. The National Association for Chicana/Chicano Studies' 2000 annual conference has attracted a panel titled, "Education Our Ways: Organizations Using Tradicion and Cultura to Develop Our Xicano Youth". The panelists plan to highlight a half dozen Chicano educational organizations including their history, programs and visions. Escuela Tlatelolco, a Chicano K-12 and college initiative founded in 1970 is included in the group of organizations.

I want to acknowledge several people who have contributed to making this project possible. Dr. Antoninette Sedillo Lopez from the University of New Mexico reviewed my Colegio Cesar Chavez research and felt that my study contributed to the literature on Chicano educational history and therefore recommended my manuscript to Garland Publishing to complement their "Emerging Voices" series highlighting the Chicano community. Guadalupe Cannon assisted me in preparing my manuscript for submission. Lastly, I thank Rachel Leona Maldonado, my wife and friend who helped and listened to me as I prepared my research for publication.

NOTES

1. Laurence Veysey, *The Emergence of the American University* (Chicago: University of Chicago Press, 1965), p. vii.

2. U.S. Department of Education, National Center for Education Statistics, *1997 Directory of Postsecondary Institutions*, Volume I, "Degree-Granting Institutions;" Project Officers, Samuel Barbett and Austin Lin; (Washington, DC: GPO, 1998), p. xxi.

3. A Carnegie Foundation Technical Report, *A Classification of Institutions of Higher Education*, (The Carnegie Foundation for the Advancement of Teaching: Princeton, NJ, 1987), p. 2.

4. U.S. Department of Education, National Center for Education Statistics, *The Condition of Education 1998*, by John Wirt, Tom Snyder, Jennifer Sable, Susan P. Choy, Yupin Bae, Janis Stennett, Allison Gruner, and Marianne Perie; (Washington, D.C.: U.S. Government Printing Office, 1998), p. 50.

5. Jose F. Moreno, ed., *The Elusive Quest For Equality: 150 Years of Chicana/Chicano Education* (Cambridge, MA: Harvard Educational Review, 1999).

Colegio Cesar Chavez, 1973–1983

CHAPTER 1

Introduction

If colleges are part of our national life, then college history is part of
our national history (p. 44).
They are threads as it were, woven into the tapestry of general history
(p. 45).
Sometimes a movement may have actually begotten a college (p. 45).
The history of our colleges and universities is the history of our
people (p. 46).

John K. Bettersworth[1]

Colegio Cesar Chavez evolved from Mount Angel College, which had
several prior institutional identities. The Catholic Order of Benedictine
Sisters founded Mt. Angel Academy in 1888 in the small rural
community of Mount Angel, Oregon. Originally chartered as a female
academy, it was rechartered as a normal school in 1897 to prepare
women for the teaching profession. In 1947, Mt. Angel Normal School
was reorganized into Mt. Angel Women's College, granting a Bachelor
of Science degree in elementary education. It received accreditation
from the Northwest Accrediting Association in 1954. In 1957, facing
fiscal problems, Mt. Angel Women's College became coeducational
and was consequently renamed Mt. Angel College. In 1966, believing
that expansion would solve the college's fiscal problems, Mt. Angel
College sought and received two federal loans to expand the campus. In
the following seven years, burdened with a million dollar debt and
declining enrollments, Mt. Angel College's future looked bleak.
Despite financial obstacles, the college continued to innovate. In late
1971, two Chicanos became part of the college staff. Ernesto Lopez

was hired as Dean of Admissions and Sonny Montez as Director of Ethnic Affairs and minority recruiter. By 1972, Mt. Angel College's student body had declined to 250; 37 of them were Chicanos.

In June 1973, Mt. Angel College received a fatal blow. The Northwest Association of Schools and Colleges discontinued Mt. Angel College's accreditation because of the college's severe financial instability. Expecting complete collapse, many faculty members and students left. In the midst of this institutional crisis, Montez, Lopez and four others saw an opportunity to redirect the institution. On December 12, 1973, the name of Mt. Angel College was changed by amendment to the college's articles of incorporation. Colegio Cesar Chavez was born. Colegio received accreditation candidacy status in 1975 from the Northwest Association of Schools and Colleges, a regional accreditation agency. Colegio represented an innovative experiment in higher education. Colegio was unique in pioneering a four year college totally controlled by Chicanos and academically structured on an educational experimental model, "College Without Walls."

Colegio Cesar Chavez was the first four year Chicano college in the West and Southwest with independent accreditation candidacy. Chicano colleges which were established earlier were affiliated with other progressive experimental institutions including Antioch College and Goddard College. Colegio was not established in isolation. Rather, Colegio was a part of a political and cultural movement taking place in Chicano communities across the nation. Innovative curriculum linked Colegio to the Chicano Movement. Courses such as "The Chicano and Social Institutions," "The Political Evolution of the Campesino," "Heritage," "Religion in the Chicano Community," and "Chicano Theater" were testimony of Colegio's commitment to Chicano self-determination and cultural awareness.

Since birth, Colegio faced critical survival struggles. The most pressing struggles during its early years were financial instability, low student enrollments, and legal struggles over federal foreclosure and accreditation. These survival struggles precluded Colegio from establishing institutional roots. Colegio's leadership successfully evaded several institutional death calls. Yet, with each evasion, the chances for survival lessened. By late 1980, the unstable Colegio was in the midst of internal political infighting which later spilled out into the Chicano community. In 1981, the Northwest Association of Schools and Colleges determined not to grant Colegio full accreditation and consequently terminated Colegio's accreditation candidacy.

In February 1983, lacking students, fiscal resources, accreditation candidacy, and strong leadership, Colegio Cesar Chavez closed its doors. In early 1986, an anonymous buyer purchased the Colegio campus and donated the property to the Order of Benedictine Sisters in Mt. Angel, Oregon. The ownership of the campus had made a full circle. In late fall of 1999, I visited the former Colegio Cesar Chavez campus. As I passed through the main entrance, a mural depicting a green agricultural field with a vivid red and orange sunset in the background greeted me. The condition of the mural was excellent. It looked fresh and vivid as though it had been recently painted. The mural prodded my memory back to the late 1970s when I first visited Colegio Cesar Chavez and admired the mural. While I was viewing the mural, a woman approached me and asked if she could help me. She introduced herself as Sister Adele Mansfield of the Order of the Benedictine Sisters. I inquired about the other Chicano murals I remembered seeing at Colegio. Sister Adele stated that the mural in the main entrance area was the only one remaining. I mentioned to her that the style of the mural resembled the work of Danny Desiga, a Chicano artist associated with Colegio. She indicated that she had attempted to find the artist's signature on the mural but could not find one. This unsigned mural is the only visual record on campus documenting the fact that Colegio ever existed. Sister Adele serves as the administrator of the St. Joseph Shelter now occupying the former Colegio campus. The shelter operates two housing initiatives. The campus's main building provides shelter for up to 12 families. The ethnic make up of families staying at the shelter includes Anglos and Latinos. The former Colegio dormitories provide shelter to single men, mostly Mexicano/Latino farmworkers.

A review of Colegio's history reveals that a slow death had gripped an anemic Colegio from its inception. This prompted Irma Gonzales, Colegio's last president to state in a 1981 newspaper interview:

> Someone will have to write this opera. Someone should write an opera about Colegio. The critics are right when they say it is the longest running death in history.[2]

I have written about Colegio to document a fragment of Chicano educational history and thereby highlight an important Chicano struggle towards educational self-determination. The story of Colegio likewise introduces the reader to a marginally known history of the Chicano community in the Pacific Northwest. More important, the story of Colegio is intricately linked to a wider story of the American experience.

DESCRIPTION OF STUDY

Focus of Study

Historical investigations of minority higher educational institutions while few and inadequate, are necessary to complete the picture of higher education in the United States. Acknowledging this sparse attention and the need for research focusing on minority higher education, this institutional history of Colegio Cesar Chavez will contribute to our knowledge about minority colleges, specifically Chicano colleges which emerged during the 1970s. This study provides insights into Colegio's founding; institutional mission and philosophy; campus community including administration, faculty, and students; and institutional life between 1973 and 1983.

This research focuses on the reasons for Colegio's closure, placing its demise into a wider social historical context. Several questions guided this research. Did reasons for Colegio's closure transcend its institutional walls? Are the reasons for its closure unique to Colegio, or were they common reasons plaguing small private or ethnic higher educational institutions? Are the reasons for Colegio's closure ones that not only plagued small private colleges, but generally affected all higher educational institutions in the United States during the decades of the 1970s and 1980s?

Colegio faced insurmountable external problems from its inception. These problems included: a decline of the private college market share; economic recession triggering retrenchment in higher education; a rise in conservatism as indicated by the election of Ronald Reagan; and the refocusing of the public's eye towards academic merit and away from equal opportunity and redressing social and educational inequalities. It is interesting to note that during the later part of the 1970s, an emerging popular view premised academic merit and educational equity as being mutually exclusive.

In addition to the external problems, Colegio faced initial institutional challenges. These included legal struggles over federal foreclosure and accreditation. These legal struggles redirected and drained Colegio's administrative energies from fundamental operational and developmental needs. After the legal struggles over foreclosure and accreditation were resolved, political infighting mired Colegio's progressive efforts.

Value of Study

An institutional history of Colegio Cesar Chavez is valuable for several reasons. First, this history will serve as an institutional case study useful to promoters of Chicano and other ethnic minority colleges. It provides an analysis of the problems that undermined Colegio Cesar Chavez. Additionally, a discussion of Colegio's accomplishments could also serve to inform other efforts establishing minority institutions of higher education. The case study will help promoters of new ethnic institutions to raise questions of feasibility, anticipate problems, and provide direction in the establishment of new and more sophisticated institutions.

Second, an institutional history of Colegio is valuable in documenting a fragment of Chicano history in Oregon and the Pacific Northwest. Since Chicanos are the largest and fastest growing ethnic minority group in Oregon and in the Pacific Northwest, it is crucial that such history be documented and circulated. Additionally, documentation of the history of Chicano colleges is important because, as Michael Olivas pointed out in 1982, all Chicano colleges established in the United States during the 1970s have now closed their doors.[3] Without documentation, this segment of Chicano educational history will be lost. Furthermore, as San Miguel pointed out in 1986, the literature focusing on Chicano educational history has been marginal.[4] It is disappointing to note that as of 1999, research focusing on Chicano alternative educational institutions is still limited.

Third, this study on Colegio Cesar Chavez and other research focusing on Chicano educational institutions will serve as an important body of literature helpful to future researchers focusing on Chicano educational history in general and Chicano alternative educational institutions in particular. As such, Chicano colleges are placed in a larger American context.

Fourth, Colegio's story will promote awareness among the Chicano and non-minority communities by articulating the social reforming role of ethnic institutions and these institutions' drive toward cultural and educational pluralism.

And fifth, the recent attacks on affirmative action including Proposition 209 in California, I-200 in the State of Washington and the

Hopwood case in Texas helps us understand more fully the challenges and barriers facing the Chicano community in the educational arena in the year 2000 and beyond. Could new Chicano colleges thrive in the present hostile social climate?

I concur with John K. Bettersworth's argument that "if colleges are part of our national life, then college history is part of our national history."[5] There is much to learn from an institutional history of Colegio. Such history will illuminate Chicanos in our regional and national life.

NOTES

1. John K. Bettersworth, "What's The Use Of College Histories?," *American Heritage*, April 1949, p. 44–47.

2. "Ailing Colegio Endures Many Death Scenes," *Oregon Journal*, 12 October 1981, p. 7.

3. Michael A. Olivas, "Indian, Chicano, and Puerto Rican Colleges: Status and Issues," *Bilingual Review*, no. 1 (1982), p. 36.

4. Guadalupe San Miguel, "Status of the Historiography of Chicano Education: A Preliminary Analysis" *History of Education Quarterly*, Winter 1986, p. 523.

5. Bettersworth, p. 44–47.

CHAPTER 2

Social and Historical Context

Animals live out their lives on an atemporal, flat, uniform "prop;" men exist in a world which they are constantly recreating and transforming.

Paulo Freire[1]

Colegio Cesar Chavez was the first independent, four year Chicano college with accreditation candidacy in the United States. It was established not in isolation, but within a reverberating social and historical context. Several forces provided impetus for the realization of Colegio Cesar Chavez on December 12, 1973. The Chicano Movement of the 1960s and 1970s; a watershed period of educational innovation in K-12 and higher education; and a growing popular ideology of equal opportunity emerging after WW II were three of these significant social historical forces.

THE CHICANO MOVEMENT

Social movements are collective attempts to influence societal interrelationships, structures and institutions. Most social movements consist of heterogeneous groups and individuals.[2] The Chicano Movement of the 1960s and 1970s adequately fits the above characteristics of social movements. First, the Chicano Movement was a collective attempt to influence societal interrelationships, structures and institutions. A fundamental underpinning of Chicano ideology was to seek "fundamental transformations in the distribution of power"[3] in American society. This fundamental transformation aimed at making societal interrelationships, structures and institutions equitable to all Americans, including Chicanos.

Second, the Chicano Movement was spearheaded by divergent groups and individuals. Activists in the Chicano Movement varied in areas of concern (education, health, politics, etc.), political ideology (ranging from Marxist doctrines to liberal pluralistic orientations), and strategy to achieve social change. Two fundamental strains unifying these divergent Chicano groups and individuals were their history and culture. Historically, Chicanos have shared a collective U.S. experience of racism and exploitation. Chicano/a scholars (Acuña 1988, Garcia 1980, Barrera 1979, and others) have clearly illuminated the historical racial discrimination and exploitation of Chicanos. Beyond this binding historical experience, language, Catholicism, music, and a common system of values likewise reinforced Chicano cultural bonds. Popular terms such as "Carnalismo" (Brotherhood), "La Raza" (The Race or the people) and " La Chicanada" symbolically and rhetorically unified a diverse Chicano community. As such, "Chicano culture represented a common ground that increased the cohesiveness of otherwise diverse elements."[4]

During the Chicano Movement, divergent Chicano organizations strived to make American society more equitable. The Alianza Federal de Pueblos Libres, headed by Reies Lopez Tijerina, sought to restore lost Spanish and Mexican land grants in New Mexico. The Crusade for Justice, headed by Rodolfo "Corky" Gonzales, advocated Chicano civil rights in Colorado. El Partido de La Raza Unida, headed by Jose Angel Gutierrez, directed Chicano energies toward establishing a political base in south Texas and the southwest through third party politics. The United Farm Workers Union, headed by Cesar Chavez and Dolores Huerta, fought against the marginality and exploitation of farm workers in California. A host of student organizations headed by Chicana/o student activists advocated for more effective public schools for Chicanos and access to America's college and universities. Numerous other regional and local Chicano activist groups throughout the U.S. brought attention to local community issues. This array of Chicano organizations seeking Chicano self-determination propelled the Chicano Movement forward.

A significant focus of concern emanating from the Chicano Movement in the late 1960s was the educational status of Chicanos. Chicanos lamented the high number of dropout or pushout rates among Chicano youth, lack of higher educational opportunities, an historical pattern of indifference towards Chicanos in the public schools, and other similar issues. In 1968, the historical high school "blow outs" in East Los Angeles raised these educational issues to the forefront. The "blow outs" involved Chicano students walking out of the schools in an active boycott. The striking students raised numerous issues including a call to end racist school practices which negatively impacted Chicano students, the hiring of Chicano faculty and support staff, incorporation of Chicano contributions in the curriculum and other critical demands. It is estimated that about ten thousand students from various schools participated in the high school "blow outs" in East Los Angeles.[5] Much media attention on the "blow outs" made visible Chicano student issues and activism.

"Blow outs" or walk outs also took place in 1969 and 1970 in numerous communities in Texas, Michigan, Colorado, and Arizona. An emerging tactic to voice Chicano educational concerns through school walk outs quickly became evident. Several publications including Carlos Muñoz's *Youth, Identity, Power: The Chicano Movement* (1989), Jose Angel Gutierrez's *The Making of a Chicano Militant: Lessons from Cristal* (1998), and Ernesto B. Vigil's *The Crusade for Justice* (1999) provide good insights into the early Chicano student "blow outs" taking place in East Los Angeles, Ca., Crystal City, Tx., and Denver, Co.

The issues which Chicano students were raising regarding public schools were subsequently affirmed by a series of five studies produced by the United States Commission on Civil Rights between 1971 and 1973. The reports better known as the Mexican American Study Report I-V, highlighted the failure of public schools in meeting the fundamental educational needs of Chicanos. These reports were significant in that they provided strong data underscoring the poor educational condition facing Chicanos.

Local, regional and national conferences also underscored Chicano activism. Two significant national Chicano conferences which moved the Chicano agenda forward included the National Chicano Youth Liberation Conference staged in March 1969 and hosted by the Crusade for Justice in Denver, Colorado; and the Chicano Coordinating Council on Higher Education conference held the same year at the University of California, Santa Barbara. These conferences resulted in two significant Chicano Movement documents which captured and defined the vision of the Chicano community's activism and future, including education. Chicano activists affirmed this vision by sharing the sentiments embedded in the words of Jose Vasconcelos, Mexican educator and philosopher, "We [did] not come to work for the university, but to demand that the university work for our people."[6]

Chicano students represented a significant group of activists who pushed forward the emerging Chicano agenda. Student organizations including UMAS, (United Mexican American Students), MAYO (Mexican American Youth Organization), MECHA (Movimiento Estudiantil Chicano de Aztlan) and others represented an emerging and vibrant network of student organizations promoting Chicano ideology and activism, particularly in the educational setting.

Some Chicano activists deemed it important to work within existing mainstream educational institutions. The goal was to change existing institutions to be more responsive to the Chicano community. One such effort included MAYO's Winter Garden Project aimed at organizing Chicano communities in south Texas to assume control of local politics including the local school boards. Crystal City, Texas would serve as the initial focus for these efforts. In order to accomplish this, a political strategy to run a slate of candidates under La Raza Unida banner in the Crystal City school board elections was implemented. Effective organizing among a majority Chicano community and a history of educational indifference towards Chicanos paid off and La Raza Unida candidates won their seats on the Crystal City School Board. An effort to transform the local schools in Crystal City soon began. A Chicano dominated school board soon implemented a comprehensive bilingual education program, incorporated Chicano Studies into the district's curriculum, hired a Chicano district superintendent and a high number of Chicano school personnel, and other important school district initiatives which collectively transformed a Chicano historical experience of educational indifference to a Chicano centered school district. Jose Angel Gutierrez's book, *The Making of a Chicano Militant: Lessons from Cristal* (1998) and Armando Trujillo's study, *Chicano Empowerment and Bilingual Education: Movimiento Politics in Crystal City, Texas* (1998) are useful resources examining Chicano Movement activism in south Texas education.

While efforts in Crystal City, Texas were focused on gaining control of the local school board to bring change in the local schools, another strategy pursued by other activists to address the educational needs of Chicanos involved proactively working with a local school district to establish a district sponsored school for Chicanos. Such efforts resulted in the establishment of "Casa de la Raza" under the Berkeley Unified School District's Experimental Schools Plan (ESP) in 1971. The district's ESP initiative involved 23 alternative schools, including Casa. Once again, Chicano activism was directed at the public educational sector. Casa de la Raza was designed to offer Chicano students an educational program free from the white, middle class biases and pressures characteristic of standard public schools. Casa was a K-12 grade bilingual, bi-cultural public school with a significant goal to engage the community in the students' educational experience. The students and school staff consisted mostly of Chicanos. Casa's governance involved staff, parents and students. The school was short lived and only operated for a couple of years due to the issue of segregation in a public school receiving federal funds. Some argued that the Berkeley School District's Casa initiative was contrary to the federal desegregation efforts which were ongoing nationally. In early 1972, the Office of Civil Rights informed the district that the Casa initiative was in noncompliance with Title VI of the Civil Rights Act of 1964. The district attempted to respond to the legal issues by revising the operation of Casa into a larger multi-cultural initiative. The plan was not accepted by the Office of Civil Rights. Subsequently, the district opted to close the Casa experiment. The Southwest Network issued the publication, *Casa de la Raza: Separatism or Segregation* (1973). This publication included a good description of Casa and a reprint of a legal discussion regarding Casa by Susan Appleton (1973) originally published in the California Law Review. Francisco Hernandez's 1982 doctoral thesis titled, *Schools for Mexicans: A Case Study of a Chicano School* also provided an excellent study on the "Casa de la Raza" initiative.

While some Chicano activists targeted existing public educational structures and institutions, others determined to create new and private institutions for Chicanos. The early 1970s witnessed a Chicano effort to establish such fledgling institutions, including K-12 and colleges. Chicanos in Texas founded Colegio Jacinto Treviño in San Antonio and Mercedes and Juarez-Lincoln University in Austin. A joint Chicano and Native American effort founded D. Q. (Deganawidah-Quetzelcoatl) University in Davis, California. Another initiative in California included La Universidad de Aztlan which operated out of Fresno and Del Rey. In Colorado, Chicano activists established Escuela Aztlan, and the Crusade for Justice founded Escuela and Colegio Tlatelolco in Denver. In the Northwest, Chicanos founded Colegio Cesar Chavez in

Mt. Angel, Oregon. Numerous other Chicano alternative educational related initiatives operating for varying educational purposes, settings, and groups added to a growing Chicano effort towards educational self determination. An early listing of Chicano alternative educational initiatives was included in *Directorio Chicano* (1974) issued by the Southwest Network. While common strands unified these Chicano controlled educational initiatives, they each had their own organizational character. A short lived Chicano college consortium brought the colleges together to address common needs and issues.

There exist some useful reference materials focusing on Chicano alternative initiatives. Two useful but brief references which highlight several of the mentioned Chicano schools are H. Homero Galicia's article, "Chicanos and Schools: A perspective for Alternative Educational Situations" (1973) and Clementina Almaguer's article, "Alternative Chicano Educational Programs in California" (1973). Almaguer's article is excellent because the author included a compilation of interviews with representatives from various Chicano educational initiatives. Both articles are included in *Chicano Alternative Education* (1974) issued by the Southwest Network. Gilbert D. Roman's article, "Chicano Alternatives in Higher Education" which appeared in *Chicanos in Higher Education* (1975) is another useful article. *Edcentric*, a periodical which was published by the United States National Student Association produced a special issue which included the article, "Cinco Exemplos" that highlighted five Chicano alternative educational initiatives. *Educacion Alternativa: On Development of Chicano Bilingual Schools* (1974) also produced by the Southwest Network served as a practical guide in establishing and evaluating Chicano schools. Juan Jose Sanchez's (1982) doctoral thesis titled, *A Study of Chicano Alternative Grade Schools in the Southwest: 1978–1980* examined three Chicano grade schools. The study concluded that Chicano alternative schools provided a viable alternative to traditional school systems which have historically not met the learning needs of Chicano children. Sanchez, likewise wrote a piece highlighting the philosophical and cultural foundations of Chicano alternative schools. The author later integrated this piece into his dissertation. The following discussion highlights some of the Chicano alternative initiatives.

In 1970, the Crusade for Justice in Denver, Colorado founded Escuela and Colegio Tlatelolco. Tlatelolco evolved from a summer Freedom School started in 1968. This initiative offered an educational experience enriched with Chicano culture and history. The summer Freedom school continued to operate during the summer of 1969. The success and experience of operating a summer school for Chicanos, the historical educational climate of indifference toward Chicanos and a growing level of Chicano activism in Denver led to the founding of Escuela y Colegio in 1970.

The documentary, "Tlatelolco" which focuses on Escuela Tlatelolco underscored Corky Gonzales's vision for the school. "We are a living image of what we say we are doing. Our school is not a factory for granting degrees and providing tinkertoy children. We are in the process of nation-building..."[7] Initially, Escuela Tlatelolco operated year around, enrolling students from grades levels first to twelfth.

Colegio Tlatelolco offered a Bachelor of Arts program through its affiliation with Goddard College in Plainsfield, Vermont. The affiliation with Goddard College benefited Colegio Tlatelolco for purposes of accreditation. The linkage of Escuela and Colegio Tlatelolco was significant in having college students work with K-12 students. Tlatelolco has gone through changes since its founding. Tlatelolco's higher educational initiative was short lived, and closed down in 1973.[8] Likewise, the K-12 component constricted through the years. As of 1999, Tlatelolco operates a year round academic program for levels 6 through 12 and enrolls about 75 students. Escuela Tlatelolco is accredited by the State of Colorado. Escuela Tlatelolco likewise operates Escuela Tlatelolco Montessori which enrolls children ages 3–4. Escuela Tlatelolco graduated eight students in Spring of 1999.

Escuela Tlatelolco represents an excellent example of the Chicano alternative schools which were founded during the height of the Chicano Movement. Juan Jose Sanchez's 1982 doctoral dissertation titled, *A Study of Chicano Alternative Grade Schools in The Southwest: 1978–1980* and Elena Aragon de McKissack's 1998 doctoral dissertation and soon to be released publication titled, *Chicano Educational Achievement: Comparing Escuela Tlatelolco, a Chicanocentric School, and a Public High School* (1999) are useful studies focusing on Escuela Tlatelolco. Both studies significantly contribute to the marginal literature on Chicano alternative educational initiatives of the 1970s. Sanchez's study is insightful because the author examines, compares and evaluates three Chicano schools. He examines the schools' philosophical and cultural foundations, governance and funding, curriculum, and the connection between the schools and their respective communities. McKissack's study is likewise important because the author compares Escuela Tlatelolco with a mainstream public school in Denver, Colorado. This comparison examines the schools' educational effectiveness with Chicano students. The comparative study concluded that an educational experience which promotes a student's culture and provides positive role modeling positively impacts student learning and academic retention. The author argued that the public school in the study has enhanced its effectiveness in working with Chicano/Latino students. This particular public school was the site of Chicano walk outs in late 1969.

Deganawidah-Quetzelcoatl University (D-Q U) founded in 1970 near Davis, California was unique in that it began as a collaborative effort between Chicanos and Native Americans advocating higher education. D-Q U began when a group of Native Americans and Chicanos scaled a seven foot cyclone fence and claimed a piece of federal land which formerly housed a U.S. Army communications site. The site had been reclassified as federal surplus land. After much effort by D-Q U advocates, the federal government transferred title to D-Q U in 1971 under the provisions and regulations of the federal surplus laws.

Shortly, Native Americans and Chicanos began to collaboratively develop the Chicano-Native American college. The college was governed by an equally represented Chicano-Native American board. D-Q U enrolled its first group of students in 1971. An early school catalog listed the following institutional objectives: "to meet the needs of the Chicano and Native American communities through practicums which combine contemporary technologies and professional skills, to preserve and develop the two cultural heritages as substantive disciplines of scholarly inquiry, to serve as a learning center for the two indigenous communities, and to bring education to the Native American and Chicano peoples..."[9] A significant challenge that D-Q U faced was a stable financial base.

In 1978, in efforts to address the financial issue, D-Q U decided to reorganize and become a tribally controlled college and thereby benefit from federal funding support under the PL 95–471 which aimed at aiding the further development of tribal colleges. This reorganization ended the Chicano element of D-Q U. As of 1999, D-Q U is an accredited 2 year post secondary institution dedicated to the education of Native Americans and is designated as a tribally controlled community college. D.Q.U's website identifies several affiliate site locations in northern California. Two useful references on D-Q U and tribally controlled colleges include Wayne J. Stein's, *Tribally Controlled Colleges: Making Good Medicine* (1992) and Norman T. Oppelt's, *The Tribally Controlled Indian Colleges: The Beginning of Self Determination in American Indian Education* (1990).

Colegio Jacinto Treviño founded in 1970 in Mission, Texas represented the first Chicano college established in Texas. The idea for a Chicano college first emerged at a Chicano statewide conference in south Texas and became a reality with the founding of Colegio Jacinto Treviño. The mission of Colegio Jacinto Treviño was "to develop a Chicano with conscience and skill, [to give] the barrios a global view, [and] to provide positive answers to racism, exploitation, and oppression."[10] Colegio Jacinto Treviño was named after a popular Chicano folk hero who actively resisted Anglo oppression in south Texas. The symbolism of resistance associated with the college was important to the school's institutional culture. Educationally, Colegio Jacinto Treviño aimed to produce Chicano teachers. In 1970, Colegio Jacinto Treviño initiated the nation's first all Chicano graduate program to produce teachers. Colegio Jacinto Treviño moved its base of operations from Mission, Texas to Mercedes in 1971 where it enjoyed its first real home. Prior to this, Colegio Jacinto Treviño instruction took placed at students' homes, community centers and local churches.

Whereas Colegio Tlatelolco in Denver, Colorado affiliated with Goddard College for accreditation purposes, Colegio Jacinto Treviño affiliated itself with Antioch College in Yellow Springs, Ohio. Funding for the school came from federal sources, foundations, and local efforts. Similar to Colegio Tlatelolco, Colegio Jacinto Treviño students worked with elementary and secondary students as part of their graduate program. Colegio Jacinto Treviño subsequently instituted an undergraduate program. The financial stress associated with establishing and operating an independent school led Colegio Jacinto Treviño to close its doors in the mid 1970s. There has been very little written about Colegio Jacinto Treviño. A study focusing on Colegio Jacinto Treviño institutional life would add to Chicano educational history in general and in particular to our knowledge base about Chicano alternative colleges. It would be interesting to know more about the circumstances and issues which led to the departure of two Colegio Jacinto Treviño leaders to found another Chicano college, Juarez-Lincoln University in Austin, Texas.

The majority of Chicano independent alternative educational institutions were founded in the southwest where Chicanos are demographically concentrated. In contrast, Chicano activists established Colegio Cesar Chavez in the Pacific Northwest in 1973. Colegio held a unique position in the Chicano Movement as being the first and only independent four year Chicano college with accreditation candidacy in the nation. Colegio's founders established Colegio Cesar Chavez to meet the educational needs of the Chicano community, and its curriculum reflected their commitment to Chicano self determination. Rather than merely addressing the educational aspirants of Oregon's Chicanos, Colegio's educational endeavor would "lead to the reaffirmation of, and in some instances, the formulation and development of Chicano philosophy in all aspects of the Chicano experience."[11] In this context, Colegio contributed to and was influenced by the Chicano Movement. To date, my doctoral thesis, *The Longest Running Death in History: An History of Colegio Cesar Chavez* (1986) represents the only substantive study examining Colegio Cesar Chavez.

WATERSHED PERIOD FOR HIGHER EDUCATION INNOVATION

A period of educational innovation in education and in particular higher education during the 1960s and 1970s bolstered Chicano activism in the educational realm. Since World War II, American society has felt the growing pains of a rapidly developing society. "Before World War II changes [in society] had been generally evolutionary; now we are in the midst of many revolutions."[12] Changes in the wider society has greatly affected higher education. The years after World War II through the 1970s represented a watershed period for change and innovation in higher education in the United States and contributed to the founding of Colegio Cesar Chavez.

The dramatic changes in higher education after World War II affected many spheres of higher education. One significant change in higher education was the increasing role of the federal government in education. This new relationship between the federal government and higher education was initiated with the "GI Bill of Rights" in 1944. The Soviet launching of Spunik in 1957 prodded the federal government to quickly invest substantial funds for university research, support for instructional programs in the sciences, construction of specific university facilities, and faculty training. The legitimacy of the federal role in supporting education was embodied in the National Defense Education Act of 1958. In the 1960s, the now established federal role in education continued to expand. The Higher Education Act of 1965 further solidified federal government and education ties. This federal legislation benefited students and institutions. The legislation afforded students grants and other financial aid programs. The Education Act of 1965 through Title III-Strengthening Developing Institutions provided funds to assist developing higher educational institutions. Black colleges, tribal community colleges, experimental colleges, and Chicano colleges like Colegio Cesar Chavez applied for these federal funds. Title III funds targeted an array of institutional needs including administrative and faculty development, student support services, institutional cooperative linkages, and other areas deemed critical to institutional development.

A second significant change in higher education was the dramatic increase in college student enrollment. This increase was influenced by the federal role in education and was directly related to the "baby boom" of the 1940s. During the 1960s and 1970s, this great expansion of capable young people seeking education beyond high school represented an enormous challenge for higher education. Higher education responded to the challenge by staging a significant effort toward mass education. The community college movement which emerged in the post WW II era, quickly expanded in the 1960s and 1970s. Educational historian Diane Ravitch (1983) stated, "In 1946, one of eight college age youth was enrolled in higher education; by 1970, one of three was a college or university student."[13] Federal student aid associated with the Higher Educational Act of 1965 directly stimulated student enrollments in the 1970s.

A third significant change in higher education was higher education's response to the dynamic social change taking place. Many American colleges and universities significantly changed their organizational structure and governance, programming and curriculum, and in some instances, revised institutional missions. College and university structures became more bureaucratic and complex in efforts to administer federal monies and regulations, and to adhere to master plans drafted by state education planning commissions. New programming and curriculum changes reflected the growing diversity of student interest and the demand for new knowledge. Educational historian Diane Ravitch cited Clark Kerr, former university president and author of *The Uses of the University:* "The university has become a multiversity a city of infinite variety."[14]

A fourth significant change was the flurry of ideas creating new instructional practices and forms of higher educational institutions. While most colleges and universities were preoccupied readjusting their administrative structures, developing new curricular programs, admitting substantial numbers of new students, and embracing the expanding federal role; a cross current formed beneath the surface. This developing cross current emerged in the form of the "Experimental College." "Experimental Colleges" premised that educational changes in higher education needed to surpass the mere changes of administrative structures, admitting more students and providing new curricular offerings and programs. Higher education, according to the founding philosophy of experimental colleges, needed to challenge and alter established practices of providing, organizing and evaluating instruction. Likewise, education was to serve the larger good of transforming society.

Experimental colleges have undertaken various efforts to expand the meaning and method of education. Specific efforts which these colleges promoted included independent and nonresidential adult degree programs, credit for living and working experiences, credit through examination, campus-community integrated education through the work-study concept, non-normative evaluation of students, and other methods of delivering instruction. These efforts were aimed at rectifying perceived shortcomings of higher education in the United States. Today in the 1990s, many of the innovations in the organizing, delivery and evaluation of instruction which experimental colleges advocated have become standard practices in mainstream colleges and universities.

In the early years, experimental colleges such as Antioch College, Goddard College and Alexander Meiklejohn's Experimental College at the University of Wisconsin blazed the road during the 1920s for other institutions to follow. At Antioch College, Arthur Morgan reorganized the college to provide students an education with some consequence. Morgan's plan was to fuse study, work and life in efforts to produce a balanced individual. In 1962, historian Frederick Rudolph cited Antioch College as, "perhaps the earliest of the progressive experiments in the colleges."[15]

The cross current created by Antioch and other experimental colleges such as Sarah Lawrence, Black Mountain and Goddard impacted a segment of American higher education. During the 1960s and 1970s, influenced by the nonconformity, a number of colleges were founded or reorganized on an experimental model throughout the U.S. Among these included the establishment of the Evergreen State College in Olympia, Washington. Other colleges in the Pacific Northwest which have been recognized as innovating colleges include Reed College in Portland and Marylhurst College of Lifelong Learning in Lake Oswego, Oregon. In 1964, a consortium of colleges including Hofstra University, Bard College, Antioch College, Sarah Lawrence College, and others was formed to offer alternative educational opportunities and to promote innovation in higher education. The consortium became known as the Union for Experimenting Colleges and Universities (UECU). In 1969, UECU became a degree granting entity in Ohio. UECU developed the University Without Walls program in 1970 as a significant educational strategy to afford people an alternative educational experience. By 1971, UECU was granting baccalaureate and doctoral degrees. In 1974, Wayne Blaze's *Guide to Alternative Colleges and Universities* listed 29 UECU consortium members. Administration, faculty and students of UECU interacted to further the experimental philosophy that challenged traditional ways of organizing, delivering and evaluating education. Experimental colleges draw from the concepts of UECU and remain steadfast to the commitment that higher education must be in a state of constant flux and change. Likewise, experimental colleges view themselves as institutions for social change. Eventhough the UECU dissolved in 1982, experimental colleges in the 1990s continued to press forward, although the energy embodied by this group of colleges lessened. The publication, *The Carnegie Classification of Higher Education* reported in 1987 that the number of experimental colleges have decreased in American higher education and that the once strong experimental college network has largely disappeared.

Colegio drew its convictions and spirit from the Chicano Movement and its educational structure from the innovations of "experimental colleges." Colegio Cesar Chavez's educational structure was built on the "College Without Walls" program. In 1978, Colegio's catalog stated, "The College Without Walls program allows the student to provide the primary impetus for their learning; to remain active in the community; and to integrate learning and theory with practice."[16] Colegio also provided the students opportunity to translate prior learning into academic credit, and instituted student evaluation not founded on the traditional A-F standard. Colegio thus embraced the nonconformity as put forth by the "experimental colleges."

The "experimental college" philosophy attracted Colegio and other Chicano colleges because it served as an alternative and antithesis to mainstream institutions in the organization, delivery and evaluation of instruction; it was cost effective; and most important, it propelled the college as agents of social change. One area of social change was the notion of extending educational opportunity to more Americans.

THE QUEST FOR EQUAL OPPORTUNITY

The notion of equal opportunity has had a significant effect on the collective mind of American society. Although the quest for "equal opportunity" transcended all sectors of society, it was most observable in the educational sphere. Gunnar Myrdal, author of, *An American Dilemma* (1944), and others exposed America's social contradictions of democracy. According to Diane Ravitch, Myrdal exposed "the gulf between what he called the American creed--which extols freedom, opportunity, justice, equality, and liberty and the commonplace practices of racial prejudice and segregation."[17] The writings of Myrdal and others significantly impressed this social contradiction in America's collective mind. In 1954, the U.S. Supreme Court faced this democratic paradox. Deeply influenced by social writings such as Myrdal's *An American Dilemma*, the U.S. Supreme Court in its 1954 historic decision, Brown vs. Board of Education, attempted to reconcile America's democratic ideals and America's social realities of discrimination and inequality. Chief Justice Earl Warren succinctly stated the foundation of the Brown Decision:

> It is doubtful that any child may reasonably be expected to succeed in life if he is denied the opportunity of an education. Such an opportunity where the state has undertaken to provide it, is a right which must be made available to all on equal terms.[18]

The Brown Decision is a cornerstone in the ideology of equal opportunity. During the 1960s, writers such as Michael Harrington, *The Other America* (1962); Kenneth Clark, *Dark Ghetto: Dilemmas of Social Power* (1965); and James Coleman, *Equality of Educational Opportunity* (1966) continued to expose the social incongruency between reality and idealism.

Responding to this continual paradox, the federal government institutionalized programs and policies in the 1960s and 1970s to achieve equal opportunity. Major impacting federal legislation including the Elementary and Secondary Act of 1965 and the Higher Education Act of 1965 directly resulted in the creation of Head Start, bilingual education, school lunch programs, as well as college and university student aid programs. Furthermore P.L. 94–142 and Title VII extended the Civil Rights Act of 1964 to include all educational institutions. Collectively, this federal legislation extended equal opportunity to more Americans and as such emerged as a national social policy in the decades of the 1960s and early 70s.

Within this context of equal opportunity, the founders and supporters of Colegio Cesar Chavez strove to afford Chicanos in Oregon an equal opportunity to higher education. Chicano author Michael Olivas stated in 1984, "Majority Americans frequently perceive equality solely in terms of increased minority access into white institutions."[19] Yet minority controlled institutions such as Colegio Cesar Chavez need to be recognized and supported as variant dimensions of the drive toward equal opportunity of higher education to ethnic communities.

As an alternative higher educational institution, Colegio Cesar Chavez was indeed expanding educational equal opportunity. In 1977, Colegio leaders stated that Colegio's graduating class of 1977 included more Chicanos (thirteen) than those graduating in all of Oregon's state colleges and universities. Chicanas also benefited from Colegio's drive towards opening educational opportunities for Chicanos. Colegio's Project Mujer, an outreach program begun in 1979 afforded Chicanas an educational opportunity usually not available to Chicanas because of economic, social, cultural and educational barriers.

Colegio's emphasis on bilingual-bicultural education afforded Chicanos higher education which valued and supported their culture and language. This bilingual-bicultural emphasis which was not present in mainstream colleges attracted Chicano students who felt disconnected from mainstream colleges/universities. Colegio's "College Without Walls" afforded the adult Chicano student a flexible educational program complementing their role of parent, student and worker. Additionally, Colegio's effort to grant college credit for prior learning experience allowed Chicano adult students to translate prior non-formal experience into college credit.

Ethnic institutions such as Colegio augment a diversity which historian Laurence R. Veysey, in *The Emergence of the American University* argued is a unique feature of American higher education. This institutional diversity serves to extend equal educational opportunity to a diverse American society.

In attempting to understand Colegio Cesar Chavez and its founding in 1973, it is pertinent to examine the dynamic relationship between Colegio's founding and the social and historical context of its time. Three social and historical forces providing impetus for Colegio Cesar Chavez's founding were the Chicano Movement of the 1960s and 1970s; a watershed period of educational innovation in higher education; and a commonly shared ideology of equal opportunity.

NOTES

1. Paulo Freire, *Pedagogy of the Oppressed* (New York: The Seabury Press, 1970), p. 88.

2. *The Politics of Mass Society*, cited by Abelardo Valdez, "Selective Determinants in Maintaining Social Movement Organizations: Three Case Studies from the Chicano Community" (n.p., n.d.), p. 30.

3. Leobardo F. Estrada et al., "Chicanos in the U.S.: A History of Exploitation and Resistance," *Daedalus*, no. 2 (Spring 1981), p. 122.

4. Ibid., p. 123.

5. Carlos Muñoz Jr., *Youth, Identity, and Power: The Chicano Movement* (New York: Verso, 1989), p. 64.

6. Chicano Coordinating Council on Higher Education, *El Plan de Santa Barbara: A Chicano Plan for Higher Education* (Santa Barbara, Calif.: La Causa Publication, 1970), p. 11.

7. *Tlatelolco*, cited by Juan Jose Sanchez, *A Study of Chicano Alternative Grade Schools in the Southwest: 1978–1980* (Boston: Harvard University, 1982), p. 77.

8. Juan Jose Sanchez, *A Study of Chicano Alternative Grade Schools in the Southwest: 1978–1980* (Boston: Harvard University, 1982), p. 41.

9. Norman T. Oppelt, *The Tribally Controlled Indian Colleges: The Beginning of Self Determination in American Indian Education* (Tsaile: Navajo Community College Press, 1990), p. 70.

10. Aurelio M. Montemayor, "Colegio Jacinto Treviño" in The Handbook of Texas Online, The Texas Historical Association, Retrieved November 26, 1999 from the World Wide Web: http://www.tsha.utexas.edu/handbook/online/.

11. Colegio Cesar Chavez, *Colegio Cesar Chavez Catalog* (Mt. Angel, Ore.: Colegio Cesar Chavez, 1978), p. 6.

12. Lewis B. Mayhew, ed., *Higher Education in the Revolutionary Decades* (Berkeley: McCutchan Publishing Corp., 1967), p. 11.

13. Diane Ravitch, *The Troubled Crusade: American Education, 1945–1980* (New York: Basic Books, 1983), p. 184.

14. *The Uses of the University*, cited by Diane Ravitch, *The Troubled Crusade: American Education, 1945–1980* (New York: Basic Books, 1983), p. 184.

15. Fredrick Rudolph, *The American College and University* (New York: Knopf Inc., 1962), p. 474.

16. Colegio Cesar Chavez, p. 8.

17. Ravitch, p. 117.

18. Brown v. Board of Education, 349 U.S. 483 (1954).

19. Michael A. Olivas, "Indian, Chicano, and Puerto Rican Colleges: Status and Issues," *Bilingual Review*, no. 1 (1982), p. 36.

CHAPTER 3

How It All Began

That is to be wise to see not merely that what lies before your feet,
but to foresee even those things which are in the womb of futurity.

Publius Terentius Afer (Terence)[1]

In the fall of 1971, the number of Chicanos at Mt. Angel College could be counted on one hand. By December 1973, however, Mt. Angel College experienced a radical metamorphosis transforming the entire institution. This chapter identifies and describes significant events at Mt. Angel College which culminated in the birth of Colegio Cesar Chavez, America's only independent accredited Chicano college.

BACKGROUND

Mt. Angel College greeted the decade of the 1970s with much creative energy, yet faced a bleak uncertainty. On its bleak side, Mt. Angel College confronted the new decade with fiscal instability, declining enrollment, and the absence of a top administrator. An administrative team headed by the school's Dean of Students attempted to steer the college through troubled waters.

On its optimistic and creative side, Mt. Angel College attempted to link itself to an apparent social mood of reform evident during the 1960s. Towards this end, the college continued to initiate and implement changes reflecting this social mood. The college's Dean of Students substantiated this by stating:

We feel we're progressive in all aspects. We strive for heavy student
involvement in all phases of the college operation and our academic
requirements are very liberal, very flexible. Open liberality is our
greatest characteristic.[2]

Some of the college's innovative curriculum reflected this
progressiveness. Courses offered included: "Black History in
Elementary Schools"; "Executive Order 9066: Japanese Internment
During WW II"; "Black Bourgeois"; "Introduction to Chicano Arts and
Affairs"; "Non-graded and Open classrooms."

Attempting to bolster its enrollment levels in 1971, Mt. Angel
College began to implement plans to recruit Chicano students. The
number of minority students on campus was small, fifteen Blacks and
only three Chicanos. The college's initial action was to recruit a
Chicano Director of Ethnic Affairs. The college hired Sonny Montez to
fill this position. Montez was to work closely with ethnic students on
campus and recruit new Chicano students. Montez and the few Chicano
students represented the small core of Chicanos that began to influence
Mt. Angel College. By the end of the first year, 67 Chicano students
were recruited.[3] This growing core of Chicanos was instrumental in
proposing new curricular offerings focusing on Chicanos, and in
attracting Chicano faculty. A Chicano, Ernesto Lopez, was hired as
Dean of Academic Affairs and another Chicano, Jose Garcia, was
appointed to the school's Board of Trustees. By the end of the second
year, 1972, there were 75–80 Chicano students, and their influence was
no longer marginal.[4]

While tapping the Chicano student pool proved successful, the
college's financial base continued to be a critical concern. In Spring
term 1972–73, the Northwest Association of Schools and Colleges
determined Mt. Angel College severely unstable financially and
withdrew its accreditation status. This new development initiated the
flight of students, faculty and administration. Within this scene of
exodus and turmoil, the core of Chicanos at Mt. Angel College
continued to solidify their base. In May 1973, four Board of Trustee
vacancies existed. Three of the four seats were eventually filled by
Chicanos, Gilberto Anzaldua, Frank Rivera, and Leonard Ramos.[5] The
President and the Chairman of the Board were both supportive of the
Chicano inroads.

On October 17, 1973, Christian Mondor, President of Mt. Angel College joined the exodus by submitting his resignation. The exiting president stated:

> Despite many difficulties and obstacles, the college will go forward under new leadership in an area of crucial need, namely Chicano oriented programs. It is appropriate at this time for the Chicano community to select its own administrator.[6]

In leaving the college, the college president recommended Ernesto Lopez, Academic Dean to serve as acting president until the college completed a search for a top Chicano administrator.

In 1973, the status of Mt. Angel College was precarious because of the loss of accreditation, a severely unstable financial base, declining enrollment, flight of faculty and administrators, and an overwhelming debt owed to HUD. Some individuals believed the college should be closed. Chicano supporters however, believed that rather than closing the college, the school should afford the core of Chicanos an opportunity to salvage Mt. Angel College by redirecting its institutional focus towards a Chicano, bilingual-bicultural institution.[7]

The infusion of Chicano commitment to salvage Mt. Angel College was hampered by possible foreclosure reports emanating from the Department of Housing and Urban Development in mid November, 1973. HUD held the mortgage on a million dollar loan made to Mt. Angel College in March, 1966, for campus construction. A HUD official reported, "There has been no payment on interest or principal made by the college in the past three years."[8] HUD officials acknowledged that there was a significant problem at the college and the situation was not improving.

In addition to the pressing financial and enrollment problems confronting the core of Chicanos seeking to salvage Mt. Angel College, there existed the fundamental challenge of redirecting the academic programs. This brought about the need to purge the existing faculty to secure congruency between faculty and the new Chicano academic focus. This juncture created some opposition from about one-fourth of the faculty members, whose background fell outside the college's new direction.[9] However, opposition efforts to solidify a power base were severely handicapped by a Chicano President, a Chicano dominated board, and predominate support from non-Chicano staff. The administration carefully handled the termination of faculty members and other college staff whose roles became obsolete to avoid any legal suits compounding the obstacles confronting Mt. Angel College.

The Chicanos and non-Chicano supporters faced the additional problem of recruiting Chicano individuals to aid in developing the college's new direction. It was a significant challenge to recruit Chicanos "to take a chance on a small Liberal Arts College"[10] which lacked accreditation, a secure financial base, or guarantee of future employment. One of the few things Mt. Angel College Chicanos had to offer new recruits was an opportunity to take part in the development of a higher educational innovation focusing on Chicano needs. Any possibilities of successfully redirecting and developing Mt. Angel College into a viable Chicano focused educational institution, rested on the recruitment of knowledgeable people (faculty, staff, administrators).

In the last days of Mt. Angel College, Chicanos and non-Chicano supporters faced a precarious reality. It is important to note that Mt. Angel's decline and final demise was linked to a national trend of decline for America's private college sector. This decline was attributed to the increased cost of education, the decreasing emphasis on liberal arts, a shrinking pool of college age populace, and a new era of retrenchment in higher education. Small private institutions like Mt. Angel College were the early casualties of this decline.

On the other hand, Colegio Cesar Chavez's birth was stimulated by invigorating social and educational movements including the Chicano and experimental college movements. The following chapter focuses on the founding and closure of Colegio Cesar Chavez within the context of these two counterpoised social and historical currents.

NOTES

1. *Adelphi*, cited by Elihu Carranza, *Chicanismo: Philosophical Fragments* (Dubuque: Kendall/Hunt Publishing Co., 1978) p. 76.

2. "Major Gap Plagues Town, Gown at Mt. Angel," *Oregon Journal*, 5 December 1969, p. 6.

3. Interview with Celedonio "Sonny" Montez, Inter-face Inc., Portland, Oregon, 18 April 1986.

4. Ibid.

5. "MAC Board Votes to Remove Sister," *Silverton Appeal-Tribune*, 31 May 1973, p. 3.

6. "Mondor Resigning MAC President," *Silverton Appeal-Tribune*, 18 October 1973, p. 1.

7. Montez.

8. "HUD Considering Foreclosure on Mt. Angel College," *Silverton Appeal-Tribune*, 15 November 1973, p. 2.

9. Montez.

10. Ibid.

CHAPTER 4

A Collective Dream Realized: The Birth of Colegio Cesar Chavez

The idea to establish this real place, this Colegio, germinated in fields and orchards up and down the West Coast. Streams of families, generations of fathers and sons, mothers and daughters, turned the soil around it, and its roots dug deep down to rock. It caught the same constant sun that burns and ages the faces of our youth. It flourished in the humid breath of crowded tents, grew faster in the months of restless summer nights. The idea and need for this Colegio developed and branched and spread until it could grow no more as an idea. Finally, it had to be.

Colegio Cesar Chavez Catalog[1]

On December 12, 1973, an amendment to the college's articles of incorporation changed the name of Mt. Angel College. Colegio Cesar Chavez was born. Ironically, a newspaper article announcing the death of Mt. Angel College and the birth of Colegio appeared in the *Oregon Journal* on the same page as the obituaries.[2] On a less somber note, the new college staged a special program commemorating the birth of Colegio Cesar Chavez. The renaming and dedicating ceremonies included a special mass offered by the Most Reverend Robert Dwyer, Archbishop of the Portland Catholic Archdiocese. The mass was timely; the birth of Colegio fell on the same day as the religious celebration of Nuestra Virgen de Guadalupe, a patron saint of Mexican Catholics.[3] La Virgen de Guadalupe is an important icon for Mexicanos/Chicanos. Among many things, La Virgen de Guadalupe serves as a champion of the downtrodden. Likewise, the mass served as a metaphor of spiritual thanksgiving for the significant opportunity which Colegio represented.

The new name, Colegio Cesar Chavez, originated in a meeting between college staff and students. Other suggested names included Colegio Che Guevara, after the Argentine revolutionary who fought in the Cuban revolution; Colegio Ho Chi Minh, after the North Vietnamese leader; and Colegio Guadalupe, after the Virgen de Guadalupe.[4] The chosen name, Colegio Cesar Chavez honored the farmworker labor leader Cesar Chavez and the struggle he embodied. Cesar Chavez and his struggle to organize farm workers received substantial press coverage in the United States, particularly in California and the West. Much of the early activism of the Chicano Movement focused on the struggles of the farmworkers. Cesar Chavez initiated boycotts and farmworker union organizing in California and then extended his efforts to other areas including the Northwest. Additionally, the majority of Northwest Chicanos came to the Northwest as part of the migrant farmworker stream during the post W.W.II decades.

Colegio President Ernesto Lopez used words establishing a link between Cesar Chavez and Colegio in the commemorating program. Lopez stated:

> Like the farmworker struggle, we are also struggling nonviolently to bring educational opportunity to students deserving a better life. The Chicano community recognizes the enormous contribution that Chavez has made toward the well being of this nation's deprived citizens. Chavez and his farmworkers faced great odds and struggled just as we are [now struggling] and will face. This struggle was founded on conviction not easily eroded. We want to emulate that spirit of challenge. We know that the struggle ahead will be a great one and that there will be much sacrifice over the years. Yet, we are committed to survive. We will not compromise our efforts. In Chavez we see commitment to a set of principles which cannot be manipulated. We see a dedication and steadfast resistance to not give in to overwhelming odds. We will not compromise or surrender our desire to better our condition. In Chavez we see a commitment to sacrifice time, energy and human luxuries so our dream may come to pass.[5]

The individuals founding Colegio Cesar Chavez steadfastly held the belief that education has the power to create something new--a new individual--which, in turn would create a new Chicano community. Cesar Chavez expressed this by stating, "Education does not change things overnight. It makes change possible and irreversible."[6] The need to transform the Chicano community from marginality to a contributing force in American society was a powerful premise on which to found Colegio Cesar Chavez.

FOUNDERS

The founding of Colegio Cesar Chavez cannot be attributed to any one individual. The conceptualization and foundation of Colegio was a product of significant and insignificant individuals, the social context of the 1960s and 1970s, and, most important, the historical and social marginality of the Chicano community in the United States.

Several individuals and groups were significant contributors to the founding of Colegio Cesar Chavez. First, were three Chicano students who displayed a sense of Chicano activism in 1971, three years prior to the establishment of Colegio Cesar Chavez. These students were instrumental in recruiting fellow Chicanos to serve as administrators, faculty and students. They pushed for Chicano oriented curriculum and they integrated the Chicano community and Mt. Angel College through cultural, educational and social activities.

Second, was President Christian Mondor (1970–73) who supported Chicano concerns and interests. Mondor's support was manifested in his efforts to give Chicanos an opportunity to develop a Chicano oriented college, and recommend Chicano individuals to strategic positions in Mt. Angel College's power structure.

Third, was Ernesto Lopez. Lopez served as the Academic Dean of Mt. Angel College under President Christian Mondor. He later became Acting President of Mt. Angel College, and after the transition, President of Colegio Cesar Chavez. Lopez's tenure, however was brief and he resigned in 1974.

Fourth, was Sonny Montez who was originally hired as Director of Ethnic Affairs for Mt. Angel College. Montez played a significant role as ethnic student advisor and Chicano student recruiter for Mt. Angel College. He later played a significant role as Director of Administration of Colegio from 1974 to 1977. As Director of Administration, Montez was a dominant figure in the establishment and development of Colegio

Cesar Chavez. After leaving the post of Director of Administration, Montez joined Colegio's Board of Trustees from 1977 to 1981.

Fifth, was Jose Garcia, a Chicano board member of Mt. Angel College. The early Chicanos at Mt. Angel had pushed for Chicano representation on the board. In this role, Garcia began to represent the interests of a growing Chicano constituency. Garcia later served as Board Chairman of the newly constituted Colegio Cesar Chavez from 1973 to 1980.

Sixth, was Jose Romero who came to work for Mt. Angel College only months before its demise. Romero served as Director of Ethnic Studies. In 1974, Romero became Director of Academics, one of two Directorships heading the newly founded Colegio Cesar Chavez. Like Montez, Romero served as a board member following his resignation as Director of Academics in 1977.

Last were the substantial number of organizations and individuals who collectively provided insights, time, and energies, and who wholly supported the notion of a Chicano college. Some of these organizations and individuals will be specifically mentioned later in this chapter.

It is interesting to note that many central characters in the establishment and development of Colegio Cesar Chavez had worked in the fields as farmworkers. Because of their farmworker experience, they steadfastly held the belief that education was the door leading out of the agricultural fields and into diverse educational fields of opportunity.

INSTITUTIONAL MISSION AND PHILOSOPHY

The essence of Colegio Cesar Chavez refracted through a prism of four realities. They included the marginality of Chicanos in higher education because of benign social neglect, the founders' steadfast commitment to provide an alternative educational experience that did not produce a sterile person lacking their own community's collective memory of culture and history, an education energized through a creative and holistic program founded on an experimental learning model, and an education that provided a spring board for Chicano self-determination to participate and contribute to all facets of society. Colegio's mission statement, philosophy and objectives delineated these notions.

Mission

Colegio Cesar Chavez Student Handbook stated the college's mission:

The mission of Colegio Cesar Chavez is to provide a continuum of educational opportunities for persons who have been denied access to higher education. [Chicano] history and culture have been denied. Thus, Colegio offers a bilingual/bicultural program through which Chicanos may maintain their culture, [and] resurrect their history. As a liberal arts college, the Colegio recognizes the value and importance of a broad-based education...by which students may acquire the skills with which to address the social dilemmas [of] poverty, racism, [etc.] Colegio . . . promote[s] research specifically regard[ing] the Chicano community.[7]

Philosophy and Objectives

As an independent Chicano college, Colegio served as "a forum for the development and sharing a Chicanocentric view of American society."[8] Colegio's educational program was "unique in bringing a bilingual/bicultural perspective to higher education."[9]

"The goal of Colegio Cesar Chavez [was] to meet the needs of Spanish speaking people in this country in the area of higher education."[10] In meeting those needs, Colegio established seven objectives:

1. Increase the participation of Chicanos in higher education;
2. Increase the number of Chicanos prepared for advanced career opportunities;
3. Develop, implement, and disseminate bilingual/bicultural curriculum;
4. Provide individualized diagnostic and assessment processes;
5. Provide systematic integration of theory and practice;
6. Establish a comprehensive research component on Chicano issues; and
7. Provide continuity between family and educational experience.[11]

Adhering to these objectives, the Colegio implemented the College Without Walls (El Colegio Sin Paredes) which allowed students to remain active in the community, to be responsible for their own educational progress, and to combine traditional classroom work with practical experience.[12]

The College Without Walls Program is an alternative form of higher education created by the Union for Experimenting Colleges and Universities (UECU). The UECU developed the concept of the College Without Walls in the 1970. Although not every College Without Walls Program is identical, implementing institutions generally adhere to a set of organizing principles. These includes the inclusion of a broad age range of students; active participation of students, faculty and administrators in developing and implementing a College Without Walls Program; orientation seminars to familiarize participants with the College Without Walls philosophy and processes; academic programs individually tailored to time, space and content; use of a wide array of resources (instruction, materials, facilities); the use of alternative evaluation procedures including the student's participation; and instructor's roles redefined to act as facilitators.[13]

These basic College Without Walls tenets were adhered to at Colegio. Following enrollment, students were orientated to the philosophy and processes of the College Without Walls Program. They were then encouraged to establish a "Comite" (analogous to a graduate committee) to assist in developing an individualized degree program. A degree program consisted of foundation courses, credit for prior learning, internship, independent study/learning contracts, and professional employment. As students progressed through a degree program they synthesized their learning by documenting their work in a portfolio (see Fig. 1).

Throughout their academic progress, students defined their educational goals and needs, developed an academic program culminating in a degree major, evaluated the academic work, and documented their learning. Participation in Colegio's College Without Walls Program excluded a linear process. Students and faculty were simultaneously involved in any arrangement of the learning process. The College Without Walls Program required students to be self-motivated and to learn independently.

An additional facet of Colegio's educational endeavor was its emphasis on integrating teaching and learning as a cooperative venture. This was structured around the notion of "La Familia" (The Family). As a member of that family, faculty and students participated in the decision making of the Colegio. Students and faculty had representation and voting rights in Colegio's Board of Trustees. In addition, Colegio's "Comite System" (Committee) which assisted students in developing,

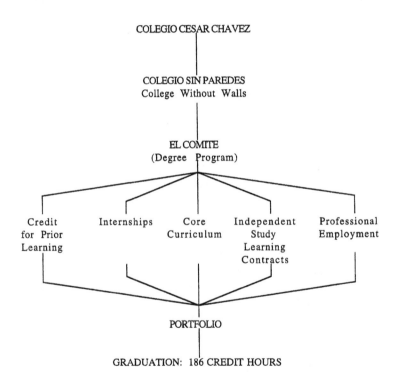

COLEGIO CESAR CHAVEZ

COLEGIO SIN PAREDES
College Without Walls

EL COMITE
(Degree Program)

Credit for Prior Learning

Internships

Core Curriculum

Independent Study Learning Contracts

Professional Employment

PORTFOLIO

GRADUATION: 186 CREDIT HOURS

Figure 1: College without Walls

monitoring, and evaluating a student's individual learning program, included faculty and student members.

CURRICULUM

Colegio Cesar Chavez's educational structure was founded on a tradition of experimental learning. Adhering to a philosophy of non-traditional learning, Colegio instituted the College Without Walls model. The College Without Walls educational model required students that were self motivating and had the interest to initiate and pursue a specific learning program independently. Colegio's curriculum reflected the integration of campus and community based learning.

Campus Core Curriculum

"Introductory Seminar" was a course designed to orientate students to Colegio's educational philosophy and the concept of the College Without Walls. "Support Group" was an in-depth seminar designed to introduce students to specific components making up the College Without Walls Program at Colegio. These included degree planning, prior learning assessment, independent study, internship, and the learning contract method. The course also provided students with group process activities which centered on common issues of career, life and education.

Foundation Courses

Colegio's core foundation courses included course work in four areas: Social Science (Anthropology, Economics, Political Science, Psychology, Sociology); the Humanities (Literature, History, Arts, Philosophy, Language); the Natural Sciences and Mathematics; and Communications (oral and written bilingual communications). Each student was required to complete fifteen credit hours in each foundation area, for a total of 60 credit hours. Required course work could be fulfilled by transferring credits in parallel areas; enrolling or completing core courses at Colegio; and receiving credit for prior learning.

Individualized Student Programs

In addition to the foundation course work, students designed and pursued an individualized program which constituted their major area of study. A student's major area of study could represent a traditional disciplinary college major such as History or a multidisciplinary major such as Chicano Studies.

A student's major ranged between 60–90 credit hours. A minimum of 45 credit hours were to be theory based and 15–45 practical or practice focused. The practice based learning could be secured through independent study, professional-intern learning or through assessment of prior learning. Some Colegio graduates received undergraduate degrees with emphasis on community organizing, bilingual education, migrant education, art/photography, and Latin American Studies.[14] By definition, individual student programs were not standardized.

ADMINISTRATION, FACULTY, STUDENTS AND COMMUNITY

A characteristic dominant in Colegio Cesar Chavez's brief ten year history was the constant flux of individuals serving as administrators, faculty, students and community supporters. This can be viewed as positive in that the organization encouraged fluid participation of individuals in various capacities. The constant flux of individuals can also be viewed as detrimental in that it undermined maintaining a stable personnel and hindered a sustaining drive to develop and implement the organization's goals and objectives. The following sections provide a profile of the flux of Colegio's administration, faculty, students and community supporters.

Administration

In Colegio's brief ten year history, four administrations steered the institution. Each of the college's top administrators had tenures burdened with substantial institutional crises.

Ernesto Lopez, former Mt. Angel College's Academic Dean and Acting President continued serving as President of the newly formed Colegio Cesar Chavez. Lopez's presidency ended one year later in 1974. During his tenure the basic issues of institutional survival continued to be Colegio's central concern. Subsequent to Lopez's brief tenure, the administrative head was altered to a co-directorship. Sonny Montez served as Director of Administration and Jose Romero served as Director of Academics. It was hoped that this co-directorship administrative structure would relieve the overwhelming duties which burdened Colegio's first president.[15]

Whereas Lopez had an advanced degree and some experience in higher education, Montez, the new Director of Administration lacked both the level of education and experience appropriate for a college's top administrator. Yet Montez's commitment to Chicano self-determination, steadfast dedication and hard work for Colegio were significant compensations. Montez's organizing ability, numerous contacts, and experience as a former farm worker with few educational opportunities reinforced his commitment to the realization of Colegio Cesar Chavez.

During the Montez-Romero administration, Colegio Cesar Chavez secured accreditation candidacy status on June 18, 1975, from the Northwest Association of Schools and Colleges. However, other critical concerns such as the struggles with HUD continued at intense levels. Montez's administrative role ended in October, 1977. He stated that his reasons for leaving included burn out, personal and economic reasons, and perhaps to give others an opportunity to lead Colegio. Montez was invited to serve as board member and accepted.

The administrative leadership structure returned to a presidential model at this time. Salvador Ramirez succeeded Montez as Colegio's top administrator in 1977. Ramirez held a master's degree in history and had been a history professor at Colegio since mid 1976. Ramirez had held joint teaching and administrative positions at the University of Colorado at Boulder and later at Washington State University. Although Ramirez had more experience in higher education, he did not have experience as a top administrator in higher education. A significant event during Ramirez's tenure was the finalization of negotiations between Colegio and HUD. Ramirez resigned in September, 1979. He passed away several years later.

Irma Flores Gonzales assumed the role of Colegio's acting president in 1979. She had previously served as staff and board member of Colegio. Gonzales's educational background included a B.A. in education and a M.A. in Psychology. Although Gonzales had served at various roles at Colegio, she did not have substantive credentials nor the experience required to administer a fledgling Chicano higher education institution. Gonzales faced significant institutional issues which were never overcome during her administration. These included developing a financial base, preparing Colegio for full accreditation scheduled for June 1981, expanding college enrollment and a period of political infighting within Colegio and disenchantment with Colegio among the Chicano community. Irma Gonzales retained her board member status while serving as acting president of Colegio. She was Colegio's last president.

Three important points can be noted of Colegio's top administration between 1973–83. First, the significant turnover of top administrators affected the short and long range stability and planning of Colegio. Second, Colegio administrators lacked the credentials and higher education administrative experience critically needed by any fledgling higher education institution. Third, important survival issues plagued each administration, directing funds, personnel and energies away from other crucial home front needs.

Faculty

Colegio's academic programs were directed by two groups; full time and adjunct faculty. Colegio's faculty consisted of a full time core faculty of five to nine instructors and a volunteer adjunct faculty of up to thirty-five instructors.

Core Faculty

Colegio's core faculty taught core curriculum, developed campus based programs and acted as advisors and facilitators to Colegio students. Additionally, Colegio's core faculty participated on the Board of Trustees, the Academic Review Committee (which awarded academic credit for prior learning), and other school committees.

Three features of Colegio's core faculty are worthy of note. First, the core faculty was small. Between 1973 and 1983, the instructional staff ranged from five to nine. The majority of the time, the faculty core consisted of six instructors. The ramification of such a small cadre of faculty members are obvious. Second, Colegio's faculty compensation was low. In an application and funding proposal submitted in 1978 to the Federal Government's Title III Institutional Development Program, Colegio stated that the average salary for full-time instructors was $12,000 per year. The 1982 national average was $23,100 for a 9 or 10 month faculty contract and $31,900 for a 12 month contract.[16] Faculty positions were basically supported by grant funding rather than from tuition or endowments.

Third, Colegio's faculty were overextended. Teaching the core curriculum, developing new courses and academic programs, acting as advisors and facilitators to Colegio students, participating on Colegio's board, grant writing, personal professional development, and commitments to critical faculty committees and the external community overextended the faculty's energy and time. This was further impacted by faculty involvement in Colegio's struggles with HUD and NWASC.

Those and other factors precipitated a high turnover of core faculty between 1973 and 1983. For example, of the core faculty serving during the 1976–77 academic year, none were present during the following academic year. In addition, Colegio hired a new Director of Academics the same year. Although entire faculty changes were not the norm, Colegio experienced constant faculty attrition between 1973 and 1983.

Faculty attrition at small fledgling schools such as Colegio has evident and substantial ramifications. Faculty attrition leads to an unstable instructional force and undermines the institution's stability. An unstable faculty obstructs the need to develop faculty leadership, faculty/student rapport, and sustained academic program planning. The reasons for Colegio's faculty turnover can be attributed to low faculty salaries, unstable financial base fostering uncertainty, and overburdening responsibilities.

Adjunct Faculty

Considering the instability of Colegio's core faculty, the role of Colegio's adjunct faculty was extremely important. The adjunct faculty was a volunteer teaching corps. Some adjunct faculty offered their services, others were actively recruited. Those recruited were identified by students, faculty, or by the community. Among the most noted adjunct faculty at Colegio were Jose Angel Gutierrez, founder of La Raza Unida Party, a significant Chicano "Third Party" political initiative in southwestern U.S.; and Alurista, a widely known Chicano poet who with literary critic Dr. Tomas Ybarra coordinated a humanities seminar series at Colegio.[17] Most adjunct faculty were Chicanos with full time employment in government and nongovernment agencies.

Adjunct faculty acted as reinforcements to core faculty. Adjunct faculty were critical resource individuals whose professional and academic background served Colegio's diverse student interests. The Director of Academics compiled a list of approximately thirty-five individuals who participated as adjunct faculty. Their professional and academic backgrounds differed widely.

Colegio's adjunct faculty corps had its advantages. First, Colegio's adjunct faculty evidenced the support for Colegio among professionals from the Chicano and non-Chicano community. Second, Colegio lacked the funding to hire a substantial faculty and depended heavily on adjunct faculty to fill teaching positions. Third, through the recruiting of adjunct faculty, Colegio acted as a forum for the interaction of individuals and ideas useful to Colegio. Fourth, the expertise of the adjunct faculty brought credibility and resources to Colegio's academic programs. And fifth, a fluid adjunct faculty corps complimented Colegio's shifting curriculum and innovation.

Yet the nagging reality of Colegio's adjunct faculty was their volunteerism. The constant flux of incoming and outgoing faculty members affected the institution's ability to sustain enduring academic programs and long range planning, and ultimately contributed to undermining the institution's stability.

Students

Colegio's mission statement declared, "The mission of Colegio Cesar Chavez is to provide a continuum of educational opportunities for persons who have been denied access to higher education."[18] Within this populace exists the Chicano. As one of several Chicano colleges established in the early 1970s, Colegio Cesar Chavez was steadfastly committed to bringing self-determination to the Chicano community through education.

Recruitment resulting from this mission focused on students who were predominately from Chicano, farmworker, and low income communities. Colegio students were generally not recent high school graduates. Rather, Colegio's students included adult students transferring from other mainstream higher education institutions, returning students, or adult students who never had an opportunity to attend college. According to Jose Romero, former Director of Academics, the mean age of Colegio's first graduating class was 32 years.[19] Although Chicanos comprised the overwhelming student ethnic group, Colegio's academic programs were open to all, regardless of ethnicity. This is substantiated by enrollment of Black, Native American and Anglo students. Colegio's first graduating class in 1976–77 included Barbara Finley Branch, a Black student; and Robin Aaberg, an Anglo student who was also the class valedictorian.[20]

Student backgrounds and academic interests were varied. One student came from an upper middle class family, was an honor student and a Portland Rose Festival Princess in 1960. This particular student's academic interest was Latin American Studies. She wanted to learn not only the history but language and culture as well. Another student was a Chicano from a low income farmworker family. This particular individual was a high school dropout or pushed-out student. Dropout because of alienation and lack of motivation, and pushed-out because the school system did not have the know how, nor the conviction to work with this type of student. This individual graduated from Colegio and later pursued a graduate degree at one of Oregon's state colleges. These two student profiles are indicative of the varied social and economic background and academic interests of Colegio.

Colegio's students were active in political and social issues affecting the larger community. Colegio students had an awareness of social and educational issues facing minorities and women, the need for reform in the educational community (policies, curriculum, etc.) and viewed themselves not in a vacuum but in a social and historical context. The social convictions of many students extended to direct participation in social movements of the 1960s and 1970s and marches bringing public attention to problems hampering Colegio's early development. One particular student viewed this social activism important enough to document participating in a march supporting Colegio as part of her academic portfolio.

The majority of students attending Colegio were from Oregon's Willamette Valley. Since the bulk of Colegio's students were former farmworkers, many came from rural communities which have substantial Chicano populace. These included Woodburn, Gervais, Hubbard, Hillsboro, St. Paul, Mt. Angel, etc. There were also several Colegio students from other states including Indiana, California, Texas and Washington. Several students living in Washington's Yakima Valley and the Columbia Basin pursued degrees through Colegio's College Without Walls Program.[21] Colegio however, did not actively recruit outside the state. Most out of state students became aware of Colegio through journals, newspaper articles and word of mouth. News stories about Colegio appeared in papers as far away as the New York Times.

Community

Colegio's community included four levels. These included the campus community; the community of Mt. Angel where Colegio was located; the larger Chicano community in Oregon, particularly the Willamette Valley; and lastly the national Chicano community.

Campus Community

Colegio's campus community was restrictive because of the small size of core faculty and student body. In addition, Colegio's academic program, based on the College Without Walls program made it difficult to maintain a sense of a campus community. Part-time and/or evening students likewise undermined campus life. This is evident in most institutions where the campus is not the mainstay of curriculum, learning, and interaction. Although there were special campus functions such as guest speakers, performances, meetings and lectures, they served chiefly to open up the college to the external Chicano community.

Colegio's hub of campus activity centered in Huelga Hall, the administration building. Most other campus buildings were not used, used infrequently, or used mainly for community programs. One student succinctly expressed, "Here we had these buildings, huge buildings! We felt as though we were rattling around in that place [Colegio]. There was no way that a small group could really use those buildings."[22] The number and size of campus buildings far exceeded the need of the campus community. Additionally, during the cold period, (Fall, Winter and early Spring) the lack of an operable central heating system caused students, faculty and staff to huddle around small room heaters to keep warm.

The turnover and small size of faculty and staff at Colegio also undermined efforts in developing a sense of a campus community. The college lacked the opportunity to develop long-standing faculty and student rapport. This is not to imply that the quality and opportunity to interact among those present (students, faculty, administration, etc.) at Colegio was forfeited. In fact, the academic structure ("comite"-committee) and Colegio's institutional attitude to operate under "La familia" (family) concept was significant in fostering active participation horizontally and hierarchically. Rather, it is to point out and substantiate that the pool of individuals with whom to interact on campus was limited.

Mt. Angel Community and Colegio

The relationship between Colegio Cesar Chavez and the Mt. Angel
Community was succinctly described in a newspaper editorial. The
writer of the editorial stated, "Colegio has been treated like a tumor in
the body of the community."[23] This editorial writer captured the
essence of a divergent rather than convergent relationship between
Colegio and the local Mt. Angel community, particularly Anglos. Many
individuals substantiated this separation in their interviews for this
study. A non-minority individual stated, "An antagonistic local
community surround[ed] Colegio. The community did not participate in
the Colegio experiment."[24] Another interviewee commented, "They felt
threatened about the Chicano population, felt insecure about us being
there, never felt comfortable with the Colegio."[25]

There are a variety of reasons for the Colegio and Mt. Angel
divergence. First, the divergence did not originate with Colegio, but
with the former Mt. Angel College. In the last five years of Mt. Angel
College's life, the institution linked itself with the student liberalism
evident across the nation. Many community people who were part of a
dominant conservative German rural community viewed this student
liberalism as degrading to a higher educational institution.[26] The
community viewed Colegio as a continuation of that liberalism.
Likewise, during the final period of Mt. Angel College, an effort was
mounted to remove the last representation of the Benedictine Sisters on
the college's board of trustees. This effort failed but the strained
relations between Mt. Angel College and the Benedictine Sisters
became attached to the new emerging Colegio Cesar Chavez.

Second, Colegio Cesar Chavez was located in the midst of a
farming community, and named in honor of a farmworker labor
organizer. This made some local farmers apprehensive of the possibility
of area farmworkers becoming organized under the drive of the United
Farmworkers Union led by Cesar Chavez. This concern was perhaps
related to Cesar Chavez' boycott organizing in the Pacific Northwest,
including the Willamette Valley. Cesar Chavez in fact visited the
campus twice during his organizing trips to the northwest.

Third, Colegio's leaders placed the struggles with HUD and
NWASC within an ethnic context. Colegio's leaders implied the image
of oppressive institutions of the system (HUD, HEW, etc.) bearing
down on a disfranchised ethnic minority. The ethnic factor spilled over

into the community and augmented the divergence between Colegio and the local community.

Fourth, Colegio was a legal adversary of the local Order of Benedictine Sisters. The Benedictine Sisters were longtime residents of the community, dating back to 1888. The Benedictine Sisters filed suit against the Colegio administration. The legal adversary status alienated some of the local Catholic German community from Colegio. In a federal court transcript, the Executive Director of the NWASC stated that he had received a letter from an individual of the Benedictine Order, encouraging the association not to grant accreditation to Colegio.[27] It is not clear whether the letter spoke in behalf of the Benedictine Sisters or an individual who was a member of that order. Additionally, the *Capital Journal* (Salem, Oregon) reported that the Benedictine Order directed a telephone campaign among residents in opposition to the Chicanos at Colegio.

Fifth, some members of the Mt. Angel City Council and the Mayor were openly critical of Colegio. Town and gown relationships were extremely poor. This poor relationship existed throughout Colegio's life. Toward the end of Colegio's existence, the Mt. Angel City Council and the Mayor pleaded with state officials to remove freeway directional signs with Colegio's name. The initial response from state officials was that Colegio was closing but not closed yet. The decision to remove the signs would have to be deferred until a later date. The lobbying effort to remove Colegio's high-way signs can be interpreted as a symbolic effort by Mt. Angel to cleanse itself by removing the blot which Colegio represented to the Mt. Angel community.

It is interesting to note that Colegio's campus was geographically located on the outskirts of the local community. This geographical location further symbolized the estrangement between Colegio and the local community.

The Chicano Community and Colegio

Colegio aimed to raise the Chicano community from its social marginality to a contributor to the social well-being of the entire community. Through higher educational opportunity, Colegio aimed to increase professional and career opportunities for Chicanos. Colegio also aimed to balance the lack of Chicano representation in the Oregon State System of Higher Education. Combined, these two factors served as rallying points which solidified much of Colegio's early support from the Chicano community.

Chicano community support came from Chicano individuals and organizations. This support was evident in their willingness to participate in marches advocating support for Colegio, their offers of technical assistance in writing proposals, teaching as volunteers and in their assistance in other work at Colegio. The most observable support was manifested in the various protests staged by Colegio. Among the most noted protests staged by Colegio were a solidarity march in support of Colegio, March 26, 1975, originating in Gervais, Oregon and proceeding through several communities with substantial Chicanos and terminating at Colegio's campus;[28] a demonstration rally to bring state government attention to Colegio's struggles, held in front of the State's capital in Salem, April 25, 1975; and an eviction protest march through the streets of downtown Portland on December 6, 1976, ending at the federal HUD office. The protests were effective in securing support and bringing public attention to the struggles facing Colegio. The image of an oppressive government machine trying to squash a small but defiant little college was made vivid in the minds of Colegio supporters by Colegio leaders.

Chicano professionals extended Chicano community support to Colegio by participating as adjunct faculty. The volunteer adjunct faculty played a critical role in supplementing Colegio's small and overworked core faculty. Several adjunct faculty lists included 30–45 individuals. Some of the Chicano professionals assisted in proposal writing or other technical assistance critical to Colegio. Overall, Montez commented that:

> The reason Colegio was able to obtain some early success and keep its fighting spirit was that we got a lot of people involved. The community was going to either make or break it. In order for the Colegio to succeed, it needed involvement of the people.[29]

In addition to individual Chicano support, various Chicano organizations in the Willamette Valley extended support to Colegio. They included the Oregon State Chicano Concilio, Chicano student organizations in other higher education institutions, the Chicano Club at Oregon State Correctional Institution, Aguila, Chicano Indian Study Center of Oregon, and a host of other Chicano community organizations. The Chicano organization that most significantly assisted

Colegio was Centro Chicano Cultural, which made it possible for Colegio to purchase the campus in 1978.

National Chicano Support and Colegio

Colegio's commitment to extend higher education opportunity to Chicanos was not an isolated incident. Colegio's actions and purpose were clearly connected to national Chicano activism. This coupling gave Colegio a national stage on which to transcend the small community of Mt. Angel and Oregon's Willamette Valley. National Chicano leaders and organizations served as conduits to place Colegio's dreams and dilemmas on a national stage.

The most significant national Chicano leader generating public attention to focus on Colegio's struggles was Cesar Chavez, head of the United Farmworkers Union. Cesar Chavez visited Colegio twice, once in May, 1974 and again in October, 1977.

On both visits, Chavez made clear his support and interest in advocating on Colegio's behalf. Chavez's visit in 1977 was the most fruitful. During his visit, he stated that he would directly "enlist the aid of his numerous friends to focus attention on the Colegio and on the needs of the institution."[30] Chavez's visits to Colegio were extremely important in that he served as a catalyst to rally support for Colegio at the local level, served to take Colegio from the local community on to a national stage, and lastly, Chavez used his influence and support in Washington, D.C. to initiate some movement by the government on behalf of Colegio.

Several other national Chicano leaders visited Colegio as well. Rodolfo "Corky" Gonzales, the head of Crusade for Justice, an organization advocating Chicano civil rights was scheduled to visit Colegio.[31] Gonzales is a noted author, speaker, and founder of Colegio Tlatelolco, a Chicano alternative educational initiative in Denver, Colorado. Jose Angel Gutierrez, national Chicano leader and founder of La Raza Unida, a Chicano third party initiative in the southwest worked as a part time faculty member at Colegio. Nationally recognized Chicano poets Abelardo "Lalo" Delgado and Alurista both visited Colegio and expressed their support. These individuals were Chicano Movement icons and certainly contributed to telling Colegio's story to other Chicanos beyond the northwest.

National Chicano organizations also linked Colegio to a national Chicano network. These included organizations such as the National

Council de la Raza, the National Association of Farmworkers Organization (which funded the construction of a solar green house at Colegio), the Congress of Hispanic Americans; and the Northwest Chicano Concilio (Chicano advocate group regionally based in Oregon, Washington and Idaho).

Non-Minority Community Support of Colegio

Although Colegio's main benefactors and supporters were Chicanos, some non-minority individuals and organizations ardently supported Colegio. Various non-minority students enrolled at Colegio. Some became Colegio graduates and continued to support the notion and mission of Chicano higher educational institutions.

When Colegio Cesar Chavez supplanted Mt. Angel College, a number of non-minority board members remained and contributed to Colegio's development. Colegio also benefited from the assistance of non-minority volunteers in critical times, including the volunteer work of a retired administrator who assisted in organizing Colegio's business office. Some of Colegio's volunteer adjunct faculty were also non-minority individuals. Bill Walton, professional basketball player who played with Portland Trailblazers in the 1970s and a member of the NBA 1986 basketball champions, Boston Celtics, came to Colegio to extend his support.[32]

Colegio also tapped into the support of Oregon State Government officials including Congressmen Al Ullman, and Les Aucoin, and Oregon Governor Robert Straub. Senators Mark Hatfield and Robert Packwood were also informed about Colegio's struggles.[33]

Several non-minority organizations and businesses also advocated on Colegio's behalf. These included the *Oregon Statesman*; Salem YWCA; City Council of Portland, Oregon; Textronix Foundation, Portland; McKenzie River Gathering, Eugene; Northwest Regional Educational Lab, Portland; Campaign for Human Development; and a host of others.

SUMMARY

Capturing the essence of a developing institution is a difficult task. It requires one to take a photograph of a moving object without rendering distortion due to movement. I have chosen to synthesize Colegio's progress through several years. Eventhough historical distortion may be present in this synthesis, the substance of Colegio has been captured.

This image depicts the founding of Colegio on December 12, 1973, its campus community including administration, faculty, students, and the outside community. All in all, the preceding narrative shows a collective dream realized--Colegio Cesar Chavez.

NOTES

1. Colegio Cesar Chavez, *Colegio Cesar Chavez Catalog* (Mt. Angel, Oregon: Colegio Cesar Chavez, 1975), p. i.

2. "New Name Given College: Colegio Cesar Chavez," *Oregonian*, 13 December 1973, p. 47.

3. Jose Romero, "Chronological History of Colegio Cesar Chavez," Personal Files of Jose Romero, Salem, Oregon, p. 1.

4. Interview with Jose Romero, Marion Educational Service District, Salem, Oregon, 14 April 1986.

5. "College named for Chavez," *Capital Journal*, 13 December 1973, sec. 2, p. 13.

6. *Colegio Cesar Chavez Catalog*, p. i.

7. Colegio Cesar Chavez, *Colegio Cesar Chavez Student Handbook* (Mt. Angel, Oregon: Colegio Cesar Chavez, n.d.), p. 1.

8. Ibid.

9. Ibid.

10. Ibid., p. 2.

11. Ibid.

12. Ibid.

13. Union for Experimenting Colleges and Universities, *The University Without Walls: A First Report* (Yellow Springs, Ohio: Union for Experimenting Colleges and Universities, 1972), p. 12–34.

14. Colegio Cesar Chavez, "Progress Report Submitted to Northwest Association of Schools and Colleges," "Colegio Cesar Chavez Graduates, June 30, 1977 (Mt. Angel, Oregon, 14 April 1978), Appendix A.

15. Interview with Jose Garcia, Oregon State Department of Education, Salem, Oregon, 9 April 1986.

16. Susan T. Hill, *The Traditionally Black Institutions of Higher Education: 1860 to 1982* (Washington, D.C., National Center for Education Statistics, Department of Education: U.S. Government Printing Office, 1984), p. 71.

17. Dr. Cordelia Candelaria, "Toward Securing Full Accreditation: Colegio Cesar Chavez Consultation with Dr. Cordelia Candelaria," 21 November 1980, Site Visit II.

18. *Colegio Cesar Chavez Student Handbook*, p. 1.

19. Romero, "Chronological History of Colegio Cesar Chavez," p. 13.

20. "Colegio Salutes First Graduating Class," *Oregonian*, 1 July 1977, sec. 3 p. All.

21. Colegio Cesar Chavez, "Annual Report to Northwest Association of Schools and Colleges," 1 March 1976, p. 3.

22. Interview with Robin Aaberg, Ms. Aaberg's home, Hillsboro, Oregon, 7 April 1986.

23. "Colegio's Aims are Valid Despite Financial Plight," *Oregon Statesman*, 30 August 1976, p. B12.

24. Aaberg.

25. Garcia.

26. "Major Gap Plagues Town, Gown at Mt. Angel," *Oregon Journal*, 5 December 1969, p. 6.

27. Colegio Cesar Chavez v. Northwest Association of Schools and Colleges, Doc. #85 Wheeling. (U.S. District Court), 37 (1977).

28. "Colegio Backers Will Demonstrate" *Oregon Statesman*, 28 March 1975, sec. 4 p. 36.

29. Interview with Celedonio "Sonny" Montez, Inter-face Inc., Portland, Oregon, 18 April 1986.

30. "Chavez Vows Fight for Colegio," *Oregonian*, 28 October 1977, p. Bi.,

31. Colegio Cesar Chavez "National Demonstration Flyer," (Mt. Angel: Colegio Cesar Chavez, n.d.).

32. Garcia.

33. Romero, "Chronological History of Colegio Cesar Chavez," p. 5–6.

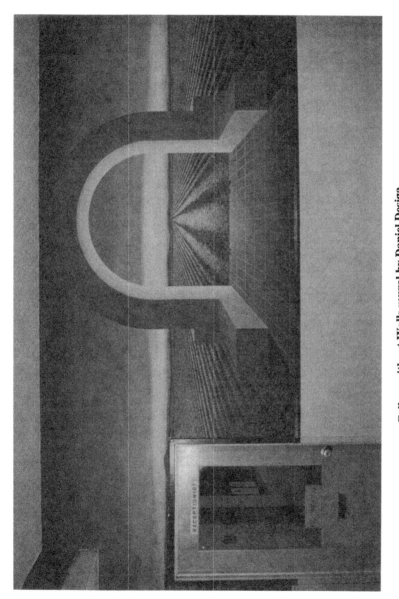

College without Walls mural by Daniel Desiga.

A Colegio classroom.

Colegio Administrative Co-Directors, Celedonio "Sonny" Montes and José Romero.

National Demonstration
In Solidarity with
COLEGIO CESAR CHAVEZ

April 25, 1975
12:00 NOON
State Capitol... Salem. Oregon

Speakers:

Corky Gonzales.... Crusade for Justice
Celestonio Montes... Director Colegio
La Ganga............. music

Support the Colegio Cesar Chavez in its struggle
to establish an educational institution for third world
and other working class people.

A Colegio flyer: Demonstration March.

CELEBRACION
12 DE DICIEMBRE

Colegio Cesar Chavez
DOS AÑOS DE LUCHA
AGENDA

PELIQULAS

11:00	-	REQUIEM 29
1:00	-	NOSOTROS VENCEREMOS
2:00	-	LUCHANDO POR NUESTRAS VIDAS
4:00	FAMILY CIRCUS	
4:30	TEATRO DEL PIOJO	
5:30	FAMILY CIRCUS	
6:00	MISA EN LA IGLESIA ST. MARY	
7:00	CENA DE UNIDAD	
	BAILE FOLKLORICOS	
	HABLISTAS	
9:00	GRAN BAILES	

DURANTE EL DIA: EXHIBICION DE ARTE CHICANA

A Colegio flyer: Colegio Celebration

Colegio Cesar Chaves: graduation ceremony.

Colegio Cesar Chaves: graduation day.

CHAPTER 5

Fading Dreams and Hopes: Colegio's Decline and Demise

Someone definitely will have to write this opera. Someone should write an opera about Colegio. The critics are right when they say it is the longest running death in history.

Colegio's last president, Irma Gonzales[1]

Colegio Cesar Chavez sought to make manifest the goals of the Chicano social movement by promoting the notions of self-determination and equity in the social community. Despite such a popular and positive beginning, Colegio faced numerous problems and issues that undermined its development and ultimately contributed to its demise. The evidence substantiates that Colegio's demise could not be attributed to a chief institutional issue, nor were the institutional problems facing Colegio equal in their effect. Collectively, however, internal and external problems weakened Colegio's chances of survival.

A LACK OF FINANCIAL BASE

Shortly before the founding of Colegio Cesar Chavez, resigning Mt. Angel College President, Father Christian Mondor stated: "I am confident that despite many difficulties and obstacles the college will go forward under new leadership in an area of crucial need, namely Chicano oriented programs."[2] Many of the difficulties President Mondor saw as plaguing Mt. Angel College cast a long shadow on the newly founded Colegio Cesar Chavez.

Colegio was in a much better situation than other Chicano alternative educational institutions. Colegio was able to secure accreditation candidacy status in 1975 and therefore was able to obtain not only federal student aid funding but also Title III Developing Institution Funds which some of the other Chicano colleges did not enjoy. Yet the school's lack of a financial base was a central concern facing the founders and subsequent individuals developing Colegio Cesar Chavez. Individuals interviewed (including administrators, board members, faculty and students) unanimously selected the lack of financial resources as a continual concern affecting Colegio throughout its brief operation.

The first problem related to the institution's financial status was Colegio's indebtedness to the Federal Department of Housing and Urban Development, HUD. Although Colegio's leadership did not incur the debt, they assumed or inherited a million dollar debt incurred by the co-obligators, the Order of Benedictine Sisters and the independent administration of Mt. Angel College. In 1974, through a complex legal arrangement between the Benedictine Sisters, Colegio, and the bank holding the college mortgage, Colegio assumed the federal debt. The bank dismissed the Benedictine Sisters as parties in any future foreclosures.

This was the status of Colegio's indebtedness to HUD until mid 1978 when a Chicano organization, Centro Chicano Cultural assisted Colegio's purchase of the campus for $250,000. Yet between 1974 and mid 1978, Colegio endured numerous eviction and foreclosure attempts by HUD. The prolonged Colegio and HUD struggle, although resolved in 1978, redirected much energy, money and attention away from the college's development. HUD's eviction and foreclosure efforts undermined the stability of the institution. This instability hampered Colegio's ability to recruit students and personnel. Additionally, the foreclosure dilemma adversely affected Colegio's attempts to secure support from other funding sources. As one interviewee stated, "what student, professional or funding source who wasn't committed to or understood Colegio would want to become involved with a college which might close tomorrow?"[3]

The second problem related to a weak financial base was Colegio's inability to hire a high caliber staff. According to Colegio's 1978 grant application to Federal, Title III or Institutional Development Program, the average salary for a full-time instructor was $12,000 per year.[4] The Chief Administrator's salary was $17,000.[5] Faculty compensation of ethnic higher education institutions has been historically lower than mainstream white institutions. Yet, Colegio's faculty compensation was significantly depressed when compared to other ethnic faculties. For example, according to Susan Hill in, *The Traditional Black Institutions of Higher Education: 1860–1982*, "The average salary of full-time faculty in traditionally black institutions in 1982 was about $21,000 for a nine month contract, and $29,000 for a twelve month contract."[6]

Acceptance of low faculty salaries can be viewed as a steadfast commitment by dedicated faculty to the survival of Colegio. Yet low faculty salaries, compounded by the financial instability of Colegio, restricted Colegio's ability to attract high caliber faculty and administrators.

Colegio's deflated faculty salaries were only part of the problem. Colegio's second Chief Administrator commented that between 1974 and 1976 (the three lean years) there were times when Colegio staff salaries were "paper salaries . . . we went six to eight months without a pay check, simply because we didn't have any money."[7] Although Colegio secured funding for faculty salaries, the salaries were deflated. According to Colegio records, most staff salaries were grant based. Cash flow was a significant institutional problem.

The third problem related to Colegio's weak financial base was Colegio's inability to adequately maintain its physical plant. Colegio's central heating system broke down in 1975 and remained in disrepair until October, 1980. Colegio did not have the funds to overhaul the heating system until 1980 when it received a substantial donation to repair the system. The lack of heat affected the working conditions of staff and students. A news reporter cited in February of 1980, "The chill of a midwinter day didn't stop at the doorway to Colegio, it followed visitors right inside and hung close. The heating system which went out four years ago is still out of commission."[8]

A former Colegio graduate recalled, "We stayed for two months at Colegio's living quarters until it got too cold. We later moved to an apartment in town. During working or class hours we used to huddle around these small space heaters trying to keep warm."[9] Staff and students wore several layers of clothes in efforts to fight off the cold. The willingness and spirit shown by faculty and students to work and learn in a cold building reinforces the notion that people viewed Colegio's survival above their own working and learning comfort. Yet, this spirit did not negate the impact a cold facility had on the working and learning taking place. The number of years (1975–1980) Colegio operated without a heating system also adversely affected attempts to recruit students and staff to Colegio. Colegio's ability to generate revenue by providing student housing and by offering conference facilities to other organizations was undermined by the poor physical plant condition and lack of heating. Physical plant structures went unattended due to the significant cost in maintaining a campus which was fighting for financial survival.

A fourth problem related to Colegio's weak financial base was financial restrictiveness inhibiting Colegio's ability to do short and long range planning, to invest substantial funds to generate new revenues by fund raising, to hire additional staff useful to Colegio, and to gain fiscal creditability among other higher education institutions. Montez succinctly stated, "We never really could grow with a one million dollar debt over our head."[10]

In the final analysis, Colegio's weak financial base stunted Colegio's ability to develop and contributed to its final demise. That opinion was held by many individuals associated with Colegio. Montez, Colegio's top administrator pointed out:

> Colegio was significantly handicapped. The other Chicano colleges like Colegio were in the same boat, we lacked the financial base. Colegio and other Chicano colleges came together to focus on how we as Chicano colleges could survive. We had the ideas, methods to develop yet the thing that hurt us was the financial base. Had we the resources, Colegio and other Chicano colleges could have survived.[11]

Lengthy legal battles further compounded Colegio's financial dilemma.

COLEGIO'S LEGAL BATTLES

Colegio's brief history endured much controversy emanating from legal battles with the Department of Housing and Urban Development (HUD), and the Northwest Association of Schools and Colleges (NWASC). Although Colegio faced other legal struggles, the accreditation and foreclosure cases were the most substantial legal obstacles Colegio faced during its first five years of development. Colegio overcame both legal obstacles, yet these legal battles detracted from Colegio's early development, and threatened its ultimate chances of survival.

Accreditation Struggles

When Colegio supplanted Mt. Angel College on December 12, 1973, Mt. Angel College lacked accreditation. Its accreditation had been withdrawn by the NWASC in 1972 due to financial instability. Colegio's founders acknowledged that the only way for the newly formed Colegio to have any chance of survival was to secure accreditation. Federal student aid and federal institutional grants were premised on Colegio having accreditation status.

Colegio leaders first attempted to align themselves with other colleges to benefit from their accreditation. Most Chicano colleges were not independently accredited by their regional accrediting unit. Rather, most Chicano colleges' accreditation was sponsored through affiliation with other accredited higher educational institutions. One such institution was Antioch College, part of the Union for Experimenting Colleges and Universities in Yellow Springs, Ohio. Colegio's leadership attempted to be co-sponsored or aligned with another Chicano college to benefit from that college's Antioch accreditation, resource information and strategy for becoming a viable institution. A Consortium of Chicano colleges met in California and then later in Mt. Angel, Oregon to carry out discussions. However, Colegio's leaders became disillusioned after several meetings and determined that their only alternative was to independently seek accreditation from NWASC. Colegio's leaders based their decision on several reasons. First, participating Chicano colleges were not well organized as a unit. Second, institutional problems pre-occupied participating Chicano colleges, hindering efforts to work cooperatively. Third, Colegio Cesar Chavez was, in some ways, in a better situation than other Chicano colleges, an example being Colegio's substantial campus.

After substantial work and lobbying, Colegio produced and submitted an institutional self-study to NWASC. On June 18, 1975, NWASC granted Colegio candidacy status for accreditation. Colegio was to submit a complete audited financial statement to the Association shortly after June 1975, yet no specific date was set. In January, 1976, the NWASC had not received the audit statement and Executive Director James Bemis sent a letter to Colegio requesting that it be submitted.

Colegio contracted an accounting firm to do the audit and prepare an audit statement by June, 1976. The accounting firm did not complete the audited financial statement until October, 1976. Colegio submitted documents it believed would fulfill the audited financial statement requirement to NWASC. Colegio later received a letter stating that Colegio representatives should be present on December 6, 1976 to show proof why Colegio should not be discontinued as an accreditation candidate.

Colegio argued its case at the NWASC December 6th meeting. On December 7, 1976, NWASC terminated Colegio's accreditation candidacy. Colegio appealed the Association's decision through NWASC's grievance board. The grievance board rejected Colegio's appeal and reinforced the Association's decision on April 23, 1977.

Colegio's only alternative was to pursue a legal route to regain its accreditation candidacy. On June 18, 1977, Colegio filed legal suit in federal court against NWASC, seeking a rehearing on its loss of candidacy and that the NWASC continue its candidacy pending a final court decision. The *Oregonian* (Portland, Oregon) reported James Bemis, Executive Director of NWASC as stating, "The suit is the first of its kind . . . adding that the Association had never before been challenged on its accreditation procedures."[12]

Colegio's argument contended that NWASC did not adhere to due process in the proceedings which led to terminating Colegio's candidacy status. Colegio's leaders added that NWASC did not make clear to them the issues Colegio was to argue at the NWASC December 6th meeting. Was it the quality of Colegio's audit statements, the delay of complying with NWASC's audit statement requirement, or Colegio's fiscal stability?

The federal judge hearing Colegio's suit granted an injunction requiring NWASC to restore Colegio's accreditation candidacy until a final judgment was rendered. The judge added, "When I weigh the hardship of the parties, to fail to grant an injunction would be a terrible hardship for the school; perhaps even its death."[13]

During the court proceedings, Colegio argued that the NWASC review board was not clear on the issues behind the Association's move to revoke Colegio's candidacy. Therefore, Colegio was subsequently confused and unable to prepare a satisfactory presentation to maintain its candidacy during the December 6, 1976 review hearing. The NWASC, on the other hand, argued that it had adhered to proper procedures.

On August 27, 1977, the federal court judge invoked a permanent injunction enjoining the NWASC from terminating Colegio's

candidacy status until a new NWASC review hearing could be held
adhering to due process. In the court's opinion, the judge stated:

> When the Association decided to confer candidacy status thereby
> giving Colegio a valuable protected interest, once the commitment
> was given, it could not be taken away without due process. Due
> process demanded that Colegio know what the charges were so it
> could adequately respond to them. Correspondence between Colegio
> and the Association prior to the December hearing would lead a
> reasonable man to assume that the issue involved was probably
> Colegio's substantive financial condition. Testimony at the trial,
> including statements of the Commission's members made it clear that
> nothing was clear. If the adjudicator (NWASC) did not know, how
> was Colegio to have known?"[14]

Thus, Colegio successfully regained its candidacy status through
the courts. The NWASC decided not to stage a second hearing, so
Colegio did not have to prepare an accreditation defense. In NWASC
policy, any institution with candidacy status has to progress, apply and
secure full accreditation within six years. Colegio had until 1981 to
either become fully accredited or have its candidacy terminated and
wait two years before applying again.

Although Colegio successfully regained its candidacy status, the
legal battle took its toll. First, Colegio invested much time, energy and
money in its legal pursuit of accreditation. Once NWASC did not
afford Colegio due process, Colegio had no alternative but to follow a
legal solution to remain a viable institution. Yet the question remains, if
Colegio had submitted a completed audit financial statement to the
NWASC earlier, could it have avoided the accreditation legal battle? It
is a critical question because Colegio had enough battles fighting HUD,
trying to survive financially, and developing a fledgling Chicano
college.

Colegio's legal battle with HUD caused much public controversy
for NWASC. I suspect NWASC's felt its public image was tarnished by
affording a very unstable college to be a NWASC participant. It can be
argued that NWASC placed itself in a strange situation by granting
accreditation candidacy status to an institution that might be foreclosed
by HUD. There were several avenues by which NWASC could have
become aware of HUD's eviction efforts before it granted candidacy
status to Colegio. NWASC could have become aware of Colegio's

struggle with HUD through individuals from NWASC member institutions in the Willamette Valley; news stories published in Oregon and Washington newspapers; HUD offices located in Portland, Oregon and Seattle, Washington; or Colegio's leadership.

Second, legal battles over accreditation compounded Colegio's institutional instability. Colegio's leadership reported in the *Oregon Statesman* (Salem, Oregon) that the college had canceled its summer session because of financial problems generated by the loss of candidacy.[15] The cancellation of summer session (if directly related to accreditation battle) prevented Colegio from generating revenue from student tuition. Faculty summer academic plans were preempted, infringing upon short range academic planning. Additionally, the cancellation of summer session reinforced in the minds of individuals and organizations the instability of Colegio, thereby undermining Colegio's institutional creditability, particularly among higher educational institutions.

Third, I believe that the legal battle over accreditation alienated NWASC as a whole, negatively influencing individuals who might have been sitting on the fence in favor of supporting or not supporting Colegio as a NWASC participant. It seems that NWASC's original decision to grant candidacy status to Colegio was in part founded on NWASC's willingness to give Colegio, a unique institution, an opportunity. Based on NWASC's criteria for accreditation candidacy status, an institution's eligibility is reviewed on whether an institution has established an adequate financial base of funding commitments. Colegio was never able to secure a financial base adequate for a fledgling institution. In fact, Colegio's lack of a financial base was a significant reason for Colegio's demise. I believe that NWASC's alienation caused by legal battles over accreditation impacted Colegio's 1981 full accreditation review. Colegio had to prove on its own right, that it warranted full accreditation, and could not merely rely on NWASC's willingness to aid a unique developing institution. Colegio's legal battle with NWASC directly affected Colegio's viability. Yet, considering a barrage of other institutional problems converging on Colegio, one may ponder whether the school could have survived, even with accreditation.

Colegio's Legal Battles with HUD

In addition to Colegio's legal battle over accreditation, it endured a protracted legal struggle to secure its campus. The legal battle with HUD involved three of Colegio's four administrations. As with Deganawidah-Quetzalcoatl (D-Q) University in Davis, California, a cooperative Chicano-Native American alternative higher education institution, Colegio struggled with the U.S. federal government. Whereas D-Q struggled with the Department of Health Education and Welfare (HEW), Colegio's struggle engaged the Department of Housing and Urban Development (HUD).[1]

Colegio finally secured its campus from HUD, yet the long and protracted battle ranging from 1973 to 1978 significantly strapped Colegio's early development and contributed to the college's final demise in 1983. This section will describe Colegio's struggle with HUD and discuss how this struggle undermined Colegio Cesar Chavez.

Setting the Scene

As a result of the liberal thrust of the 21st Ecumenical Council of Rome, 1963–1965, Catholic colleges and universities have been rapidly divesting themselves of clerical control. The majority of Catholic college boards are constituted of lay trustees.[17]

In 1965, Mt. Angel College gained institutional autonomy from the Order of Benedictine Sisters. Lay governance supplanted the Benedictine Sister's control of the board. The Benedictine Sisters however, remained active in the college's affairs through representation on the Board of Trustees, fiscal support and in kind services.

In 1966, hoping to upgrade Mt. Angel College and increase enrollments, the Benedictine Sisters and the college's independent Board of Trustees sought and secured a one million dollar federal loan under HUD's College Housing Program. Thus, the Benedictine Sisters and the layboard became co-obligators on the federal loan. The loan enabled Mt. Angel College to construct three dormitories and a student union building.[18]

In the late 60s and early 70s, Mt. Angel College experienced fiscal problems attributed to declining enrollments, increasing cost of education, and burdensome payments connected with the federal loan. The *Appeal-Tribune* (Silverton, Oregon) in 1973 cited a HUD representative, "There have been no payments on the interest or principle made by the college in the past three years."[19]

HUD granted several moratoriums of principle payments during these years, in hopes that these would aid the college in regaining its fiscal stability.[20] In November, 1973, HUD began "looking into the possibility of foreclosure and acquiring title to the buildings involved."[21] Such was the status of the HUD loan when Colegio Cesar Chavez began on December 12, 1973. Former Colegio administrator and board member, Jose Romero lamented that thirty days after Colegio's birth, the "bill collector (HUD) was at the door."[22] In the following five years, the Colegio and HUD struggle taxed Colegio tremendously and contributed to undermining the unique fledgling Chicano higher education institution.

The Struggle

In 1974, Colegio submitted several proposals to HUD in efforts to halt any move by HUD to foreclose on the college. HUD rejected these proposals and produced a counter proposal. Colegio's frustrated officials responded:

> While attempting to create an illusion that they [HUD] were negotiating, HUD officials have . . . ignored [Colegio's] proposals and failed to explain why [those] proposals are unworkable. HUD seemed determined to dictate terms of the proposal, rather than to negotiate.[23]

In frustration, Colegio filed a racial discrimination suit in federal court. Colegio charged HUD with rendering differential treatment toward the former Mt. Angel College and the newly founded Colegio. Colegio supported this charge by citing the loan payment moratorium afforded the Benedictine Sisters and Mt. Angel College.[24]

In turn, HUD filed foreclosure suit on Colegio in Marion County District Court. In October of 1974, HUD's foreclosure suit was temporarily halted after HUD, the Benedictine Sisters, and Colegio reached a complex settlement. The legal settlement required that Colegio pay $30,000 in three separate scheduled payments Of $10,000, beginning in October, 1974 and ending in June 1975. After two years, Colegio would assume the HUD loan. The agreement dismissed the Benedictine Sisters as party to any future foreclosure litigation. If Colegio failed to meet any of the scheduled payments, HUD and the US Bank of Oregon would foreclose immediately. Although this legal arrangement allowed Colegio to continue to operate, it committed a fledgling institution to a critical financial indebtedness for many years.

In March 1975, Colegio failed to meet the second of the $10,000 payments. HUD sought immediate foreclosure and possession of disputed facilities. Colegio was banking on HEW Student Financial Aid Funds, earmarked for the college, to meet its HUD obligations. As foreclosure seemed eminent, Colegio began to seek community support to counter any foreclosure or eviction attempts by HUD. Colegio supporters staged marches, demonstrations, and occupied Colegio's main building. Colegio supporters marched from Centro Chicano Cultural near Gervais to Colegio's campus, held a rally at the steps of the state capital building, a 24 hour vigil at Colegio and demonstrations at HUD's Portland and Seattle offices. Many of Colegio's tactics paralleled activities staged at D.Q. University in Davis, California. As a result of these events, attention was focused on Colegio's dilemma. Colegio found support in state politicians, Chicano organizations, YWCA (Salem, Oregon), City of Portland, and a list of others.

Colegio began to advocate the dismissal of HUD loans, that the property be determined surplus and granted to Colegio Cesar Chavez. Such strategy had been successful for D.Q. University in Davis, California, and the Chicano Indian Study Center of Oregon (CISCO) based at the vacated grounds of Camp Adair between Corvallis and Monmouth, Oregon. HUD however, remained committed to foreclosure and rejected Colegio's surplus proposal. A HUD official cited in the *Capital Journal* (Salem, Oregon), " [I] doubt that the sheer political pressure can turn the situation around. The government has done everything it could to save the school."[25]

Colegio's Chief Administrator, Sonny Montez stressed that "Colegio supporters are committed to non-violence, but we stand ready to resist any type of eviction."[26] After bringing much attention to Colegio through the media, demonstrations, and marches, Colegio leaders received summons to Washington, D.C. to meet with HUD officials. Colegio met with HUD's Undersecretary, two Deputy Secretaries, Housing Management Staff and several legal counsels.[27] Two national organizations based in Washington, D.C., the National Council of La Raza and the Congress of Hispanic Americans, extended their support to Colegio.[28]

HUD and Colegio reached no final resolution. HUD contended that it needed to foreclose on the property yet would not strive for eviction, allowing Colegio to develop a plan of action. In addition, if foreclosure was secured by HUD, HUD might consider leasing the property back to Colegio. On May 27, 1975, a Marion District Court Judge signed HUD's final foreclosure order. On July 23, 1975, the federal government submitted the sole bid for the purchase of Colegio during a foreclosure sale. Under Oregon law, property owners have one year to redeem a mortgage before the owners loose legal rights to a foreclosed property. Colegio's mortgage redemption period terminated in August, 1976. During the redemption period, no new lease arrangement nor any other negotiation altered the foreclosure order.

At the end of Colegio's redemption period in August of 1976, Colegio received a letter from Assistant Secretary James Young, HUD, Washington, D.C. In sum, the letter instructed Colegio to "peaceably vacate the property prior to the scheduled start of the 1976 fall semester."[29] Colegio vowed to stay and continued generating public attention and support. As evidence of its intent to remain, Colegio began its academic year 1976–77 and staged a solidarity march through downtown Portland in December, 1976. Colegio held a press conference after the solidarity march. Montez remarked at the press conference:

> There is no way that HUD is going to ramrod this through. We are going to stay open. Colegio will never be closed. There are too many people involved. The power of the people will get us what we deserve.[30]

HUD proceeded to sell the campus at a public auction to recoup monies used in guaranteeing the mortgage. A HUD official was quoted in the *Oregon Statesman* (Salem, Oregon), "If a bidder is found, eviction would be necessary and such action would be turned over to Marion County Sheriff's Department."[31]

Relationships between Colegio and HUD continued to deteriorate as the new year began. HUD representatives visited Colegio to do an inspection. According to Colegio, no one with institutional authority was at Colegio when the HUD inspection team came, and no prior arrangement between HUD and Colegio concerning inspection had been made. Therefore, HUD inspectors were not allowed to carry out their task. A regional HUD official quickly responded, informing Colegio of the denial of access, and that Colegio had refused HUD duplicate keys to the campus buildings. Unless access and duplicate keys were granted to HUD, HUD would seek eviction. Colegio quickly responded, "Buy your own set of keys." Colegio reported that its facility required 300 keys, to provide duplicates would cost $600.[32] HUD volleyed back with an eviction target date of March 15, 1977. Additionally, HUD scheduled an auction in early March, 1977. HUD received no bids for Colegio by the auction date. This resulted in the March 15, 1977 eviction date lapsing with no new word as to HUD's plan to evict Colegio.

The newly elected Carter Administration continued the on-again, off-again pattern of eviction threats. Perhaps HUD awaited the new Carter Administration's opportunity to review and provide a plan of action. The new Carter Administration appointed Patricia Harris as HUD's new top administrator. There was still no word of HUD's eviction plan by June 1977.

Meanwhile, Colegio entered a legal battle with the Northwest Association of Schools and Colleges over termination of Colegio's accreditation candidacy status in June of 1977. Within this legal turmoil and instability, Colegio graduated its first graduating class. The occasion served as a rallying point for Colegio to persevere and continue striving toward self-determination. Sonny Montez, Colegio's Director of Administration alluded to the HUD and Colegio struggle during commencement speeches, "We are part of history tonight. This school should not exist, but it does exist. There is no way that they will ever take this college away from us."[33]

During the hot summer months, Colegio hoped that Patricia Harris, a black democrat, would adhere to her earlier commitment that under her direction, HUD would insure that minorities would be heard.[34] That summer Colegio made plans for academic year 1977–78. On September 20, 1977, HUD officials moved to evict Colegio on October 20, 1977. Colegio leaders responded:

> The eviction notice is the government saying that it is not impressed with the faith, dedication, time and money expended to keep [this] tiny institution alive since 1973. Our government is saying that it will not be impressed with the importance of this little college until we are not only willing to risk our lives [but] face marshal dogs and shotguns, tear gas and state police.[35]

On October 3, 1977, Sonny Montez, who had been a central character in Colegio's founding and subsequent struggles stepped down as Colegio's top administrator. Upon reflection, Montez stated in an interview that his resignation was attributed to fatigue, personal economics, and the need to infuse the troubled institution with fresh blood.[36] Salvador Ramirez, a Colegio professor took over leadership. The leadership of Colegio returned to a college presidency model rather than a co-directorship. Determined to continue, Colegio commenced its fall term on October 4, 1977, sixteen days before the scheduled eviction. The *Oregon Statesman* (Salem, Oregon) reported that there was "some sense of limbo expressed by students, "we don't know what the future would be."[37]

After reassessing the situation, Colegio adopted a strategy to defy the October 20 eviction date. Colegio students and supporters began an occupation of Colegio. In the midst of eviction, Cesar Chavez, President and founder of the United Farmworkers Union, visited Colegio and vowed his active support. The will of Colegio's leadership and support was significantly reinforced by Chavez. Chavez symbolized the apex of struggle and victory. Chavez's advocacy moved Colegio's dilemma from a local community to a national stage. Colegio also began legal efforts to halt eviction. Legal efforts included halting the eviction order at the Marion County District Court and initiating a federal suit in which six Colegio students argued that the eviction denied them their right to education.

The Marion County District Court rejected Colegio's legal efforts and Colegio appealed eviction orders to the Oregon Supreme Court. The Supreme Court temporarily halted the eviction order while deliberating whether to hear or reject the case.

The federal suit brought on by Colegio students was thrown out on the grounds that it would not likely succeed. Meanwhile, the Supreme Court decided to hear the eviction appeal, but required Colegio to place a $50,000 bond as guarantee to protect Colegio buildings from possible vandalism caused by student occupation.

Colegio's attorney, Don Willner, argued that Colegio Cesar Chavez was a legal tenant and therefore had legal tenant rights. Adhering to these rights, eviction orders issued at the County District Court should have been given a full trial hearing, and not summarily decided, as was the case. On February 14, 1978, the Oregon Supreme Court voted 7 to 0 in favor of Colegio. As argued by Colegio's attorney, the judgment stated that under the Oregon Tenant Law, Colegio could not be evicted without a full hearing. HUD retreated and assessed its options. In March, 1978, HUD determined to resume a new eviction legal battle. Colegio responded, "HUD is determined to destroy us and has certainly embarked upon a considerable undertaking."[38]

Although Colegio's legal victory brought Colegio immediate reprieve, the question remained, for how long. That answer came in the old adage, "It is the darkest right before the dawn." This was poetically fitting for Colegio. Centro Chicano Cultural and Colegio began talks that enabled Colegio to purchase the campus. Colegio relayed this information to HUD. Facing a possible prolonged legal battle evicting Colegio, HUD immediately took Colegio's proposal under advisement. Colegio negotiated an arrangement with Centro Chicano Cultural that enabled Colegio to purchase the campus with money ($190,000) Centro received from a land sale. By early summer, HUD and Colegio reached a sale agreement in which Colegio would purchase the campus for $250,000. The money would be forthcoming from a $190,000 escrow account arranged by Centro Chicano Cultural and Colegio. Property payments would be directly made from the escrow account to HUD.

On July 4, 1978, in a formal press conference in Portland, Oregon, HUD Secretary, Patricia Harris stated, "This [Colegio] is a unique institution . . . we hope the agreement will help stabilize the college's operation."[39] (Harris was in Portland to speak at the NAACP National Convention along with Benjamin Hooks, head of NAACP.) July 4th, Independence Day, seemed to be fitting for the press conference, for Colegio was now free from HUD's protracted and insistent legal efforts to evict Colegio Cesar Chavez.

HUD and Colegio Struggles Undermined Colegio

In the summer of 1978, Colegio Cesar Chavez resembled a NASA rocket sitting on the launch pad, presumably ready to be fired up. Colegio had successfully survived its legal battles with the Northwest Association of Schools and Colleges and HUD. When it came time to fire Colegio's boosters, the rocket shook, roared and shuddered in anticipation. Yet, as the count-down ended, there was only a puff of smoke and a whimper. Colegio was not all well. Colegio and HUD legal battles had significantly undermined Colegio's early development in a number of substantial ways. This section identifies and discusses the effects of the HUD and Colegio battle which ultimately contributed to the demise of Colegio Cesar Chavez.

The Colegio and HUD struggle greatly damaged Colegio's institutional stability. Throughout the struggle, Colegio lacked a legal principle on which to stand to preclude a HUD eviction indefinitely. The reason Colegio was able to remain on the campus can be attributed to HUD's indecisiveness resulting in, as one reporter put it, "fumbling and bumbling" the whole affair; the District Judge's failure to afford due process under the Oregon Tenant Law; Colegio's political pressure staged by supporters; and Colegio's determination to defy eviction through legal means. Colegio's institutional stability could not be achieved as long as Colegio did not have a site guaranteeing its continuation. Colegio did not have a financial base to purchase its campus, much less assume a one million dollar loan. The only reason Colegio was successful in purchasing the campus was by way of a third party, Centro Chicano Cultural. Colegio's lack of a legal principle to preclude eviction kept Colegio in limbo. A student gave an interesting description of this sense of uncertainty: "I found the turmoil quite stimulating. It was a learning and exciting experience which placed me in the middle of I advocating for my own education."[40] No doubt the turmoil was an educational experience and a fight to gain access to education, yet the Colegio and HUD struggle destabilized the institution from 1973 to 1978.

The Colegio and HUD struggle depleted Colegio's resources. Colegio expended tremendous amount of time, energy and money battling HUD. The amount of resources required to mount a protracted five year legal battle was staggering. For a small, newly founded and economically strapped college like Colegio, the legal fees exhausted Colegio's fiscal resources. In addition to legal fees, Colegio expended substantial monies for travel when lobbying the HUD case in Washington, D.C. and for other expenditures related to the HUD issue.

Besides monetary expenditures, Colegio's personnel was heavily taxed. The HUD issue fully occupied three of Colegio's four administrations. Perhaps Colegio's top administrator, Montez, best described the battle fatigue. "The reason I resigned was that I was totally out of gas. I was drained."[41] Colegio's leaders were substantially taxed in fighting HUD and bringing public attention to Colegio's eviction struggles.

Colegio also suffered repercussions in student enrollments. HUD's on-again, off-again protracted eviction attempts discouraged some from enrolling at Colegio. Jose Romero, Director of Academic Affairs reflected, "It was difficult convincing people that [we were] there to stay while HUD routinely put out information about foreclosure and eviction."[42] A consultant, doing an institutional evaluation of Colegio in 1980 reinforced that "enrollment problems can be directly traced to Colegio's struggle with HUD."[43] Two Northwest Association of Schools and Colleges evaluators echoed the same argument. In their institutional evaluation report to NWASC in 1978, the evaluators reported that the legal litigation with HUD had a detrimental effect on recruitment.[44] Colegio's projected enrollment goals during the years of the HUD controversy were never met.

Another poignant observation NWASC evaluators made was that the HUD issue "absorb[ed] much time and energy in crisis management, survival issues and legal problems. This has detracted from attention available for educational and operational needs."[45] Colegio's legal battles preempted critical needs at the home front. Policy development, faculty issues, institutional planning and other essential areas became secondary to the survival battle with HUD. A Colegio official remarked, "There has been a lack of classes and other academic programs because of . . . so much time being spent to save the college from foreclosure."[46] This detraction from daily operations was critical since Colegio was attempting to develop innovative ideas such as the College Without Walls and their emphasis on bilingual and bicultural education. Attempting to implement these ideas in a developing institution beset by turmoil was a tremendous task. Jose Garcia, former Colegio Board Chairman lamented, "There were just too many issues converging on Colegio."[47] These issues distracted Colegio to the point that when the HUD issue was resolved, Colegio was in a catch-up game to meet institutional development critical for full accreditation.

It can be argued that HUD's protraction and indecisiveness was a possible tactic to slowly starve Colegio and drain its human and fiscal resources. As was the case with Colegio's legal problems over accreditation, the HUD legal issue militated Colegio's ability to generate funds through grants. Jose Santana, Colegio board member stated, "All this publicity by HUD is undermining our efforts of attracting grants. The announcement by HUD on the sale of Colegio is an excellent example of this undermining."[48] Funding units must have seriously considered Colegio's state of limbo with HUD as a strong indication of institutional instability. Prior to 1978, Colegio's survival efforts focused on dealing with external issues. Once the accreditation candidacy and HUD issues were resolved, internal conflicts began to hinder Colegio's survival.

INTERNAL POLITICS AND CONFLICT

In the summer of 1978, Colegio's dream was closer to being realized than in any other time before or after. Colegio had endured the legal woes with NWASC and HUD. Colegio's President Ramirez, spoke on the Colegio and HUD agreement, "This knocks down the last of the blockades to Colegio's full development."[49] As Colegio entered a new period in its life, there was reason for optimism. Colegio's leaders had been steadfast in their commitment to found and develop a Chicano college. Their steadfast commitment against great odds had demonstrated their resolve and tenacity to keep moving forward. However, as Colegio entered its second phase, 1978–1983, the external forces moving to undermine Colegio were replaced by internal political fighting. This section discusses the internal conflicts related to President Ramirez's resignation, the termination of the women's project director and the presidential search which served as examples of infighting and contributed to Colegio's eventual demise.

President's Resignation

Significant internal problems began soon after the Colegio and HUD settlement in 1978. Colegio's top administrator, Salvador Ramirez resigned under fire in 1979, leaving the presidency vacant. During the second quarter of 1979–80, a consultant's report cited that the president "sort of leaves, the president resigns unofficially but then returns."[50] During the proceeding quarter, the consultant cited that "a board meeting [was] held to deal with President's role and conduct . . . a second meeting scheduled for the same topic end[ed] with the board's dismissal of Salvador."[51] Interviews with former board members indicated that a difference of ideas between the board and president existed.

Montez, former Director of Administration and later board member, reflected on the conflict:

> [The president] had basically bad mouthed some of the board members and had convinced most of the staff that there should be two camps. That we [the board] were the enemy, because we would not allow certain creative stuff to take place at the Colegio.[52]

Ramirez's stand to polarize the administration and instructional staff from the Board of Trustees was perhaps influenced by his past socialization as faculty member (at Washington State University, University of Colorado and at Colegio Cesar Chavez). I speculate that this socialization influenced Ramirez to view institutional issues from a faculty perspective rather than an administrative perspective.

Ramirez's departure created some problems. First, the transition of Colegio's top administrators for a fourth time in less than seven years invited outsiders to ponder what was going on at Colegio. The transition reinforced the pattern of discontinuity at the top leadership position, established by the first president. Second, the notion of polarization between Colegio's staff and the board solidified. This polarization, though for different reasons, reappeared during Gonzales's administration.

Third, the ideas and leadership of a new administrator would have to be defined and implemented. Time began to infringe upon the timeline for Colegio's full accreditation review in 1981, a "do or die" situation for Colegio. Progress rather than regression was critical.

When Irma Gonzales took the helm as Acting President in 1979, Colegio's growing internal problems became acute. Internal problems became evident within the staff, within the board, between staff and board, and eventually within the community. Jose Garcia, former Colegio Board Chairman succinctly stated:

> When we got the accreditation and the buildings, now we have to prove ourselves. Now the work begins. We can't go out and yell at anybody anymore. We have to produce ourselves. Now the real struggle begins. It sure as hell did, we started to struggle just between us [sic].[53]

Project Director Termination

In 1980, Colegio became embroiled in another internal controversy exposing serious internal weaknesses in staff, administration, and board relationships. The internal controversy involved a Colegio staff member in charge of a project aimed at integrating low income Chicanas into an educational path at Colegio. The director was terminated on various grounds. The crux of this episode is not to focus on the termination per se, but on the issues to which the termination gave light. These issues exposed serious internal problems at Colegio and contributed to hampering institutional progress, eroding institutional credibility among outsiders, and subsequently leading to Colegio's demise.

The termination case came to a head after the program director and two additional staff members made an impromptu presentation to Colegio's Board of Trustees. Their presentation focused on institutional weaknesses infringing upon their roles as staff members. A critical point of departure was the Board of Trustees' willingness to hear the staff members' concerns. In doing so, the board ignored the authority and role of Colegio's administration. The board infringed upon the administration's role of directing and resolving staff related problems. The case at hand points to the administration's apparent lack of attention to staff related needs and problems or to the lack of administrative control of its subordinates. Shortly after, the project director was terminated. The termination was based on the director's alleged deficient job performance and undermining of lines of authority and communication, as evident in the staff's presentation to the board. The two other staff members' services were discontinued at the end of their contracts.

The internal problem did not end; the terminated project director challenged the dismissal. A central issue arising from the resulting grievance was that the cited transgressions were due to the absence of well defined hiring and personnel practices at Colegio. Colegio had an old personnel policy manual that was being updated, however, in the words of the Academic Dean, the manual had "not been distributed in the past to the staff."[54]

The project director's termination became a legal question and was presented to Colegio's Board of Trustees. After extensive review, the board voted on several motions relating to the director's termination. Board minutes revealed a that split existed in the board between upholding the termination and reinstating the terminated director. After several failed motions, a motion to uphold the termination and yet recognize the inadequacy of hiring and personnel procedures at Colegio was passed by a margin of one vote.[55] This narrow vote exposed a split in the board's convictions on how to deal with the situation.

Colegio's administration later reported to the board that the terminated director had contacted the agency funding the women's project. The agency responded by threatening to cut off the funding. After quick negotiations with the funding agency, Colegio successfully saved its funding but at a significant reduction. The second year funding was cut by 40%.[56]

The above narrative exposes serious internal problems existing at Colegio. First, it indicates the board's usurpation of the administration's role in handling staff problems. This placed the administration in a difficult situation with the board and the involved staff. Second, the whole episode generated additional inter-staff problems. The involved staff members were ostracized,[57] creating strained working conditions and undermining the need for staff to work cooperatively. Third, it harmed Colegio's credibility to the extent that the funding agency sponsoring the women's project not only reduced their funding but threatened to cut the grant completely. It would be interesting to know to what extent this episode circulated among the funding community. In addition, since the termination hit the local papers, the local community and perhaps the Northwest Association of Schools and Colleges would have taken note of the episode. The NWASC did cite Colegio's hiring and personnel policies as an area of deficiency on the 1981 accreditation review.[58] The internal conflicts continued to increase and spread out to the Chicano community.

Presidential Search

Colegio's presidential selection process initiated further internal problems between Colegio's staff and the board, and within the board itself. The effects of the internal infighting hampered Colegio's ability to focus on critical issues such as the upcoming accreditation review, recruiting students, developing a fiscal base, and others.

Colegio Cesar Chavez seriously considered initiating a presidential search in early spring of 1980. Following Ramirez's resignation in 1979, Irma Gonzales, a Colegio board member and secretary, became Acting President. In June 1980, Colegio began a formal drive towards a presidential search. The board formed a presidential search committee, and produced a frame work delineating the search committee's functions, responsibilities and procedures. The search committee disseminated a vacancy announcement and a number of applicants responded. The presidential search culminated October 1, 1980 when Colegio's board interviewed two final presidential candidates. Colegio board minutes between June and September 23, 1980, revealed that although Colegio's Board of Trustees was moving ahead in its presidential search, many issues concerning the final selection of a president remained unresolved. These unresolved issues created much internal conflict within the board, between the administration and the board, and between staff and the board. This conflict hampered Colegio's progress not only in the presidential search but in other critical areas needing attention.

The unresolved issues were varied. Some board members felt that the search committee needed to speed up the process. Others felt that the board was moving too fast on such a serious issue. Some members were concerned that there were insufficient applicants, and that the college lacked institutional resources to fund the president's position. Others questioned the need of a presidential search when Colegio had an acting president presumably doing an adequate job. There were those who felt that the search was premature, and that the board was not clear on what mandate or direction to give a new president. There was controversy over whether the committee had adhered to the board's mandated rules for the presidential search and if the search should be continued. A clear division of "camps" arose within the board, affecting the deliberations of critical issues. Some board members felt the need to postpone or table the presidential search until after accreditation review in 1981.

Thus, between June and September of 1980, fundamental and critical issues needed attention and resolution. Yet, in a narrow vote of 5 to 4, Colegio's board ruled to proceed to the next step of the search, interviewing the two final candidates on October 1, 1980.

With the selection of two final candidates, Colegio's internal conflicts left the board room and engulfed Colegio's staff. Before the interviews, eleven out of twelve staff members presented the two candidates a memorandum indicating the staff's (those signing the memorandum) view on hiring a president. The following are excerpts of that memorandum:

> All of us support the continuation of Irma Gonzales as Acting President of Colegio.
>
> [This memo illustrates] our strong opposition to the decision of some of the Colegio board members to continue to proceed with the hiring process before completion of the accreditation process.
>
> ...you have been placed in the middle of an ongoing controversy. Your continued participation in the hiring process initiated by some members of the board will heighten that controversy.
>
> [We] question the integrity and ability to make sound judgment on the part of board members who requested your presence in hiring sessions at this time.[59]

When the presidential interview date arrived, the board decided to record and transcribe the interview proceedings of the two presidential finalists, Jose Angel Gutierrez and Reymundo Marin. The interview document was significant in gaining insights into the interview proceedings. The interview proceedings document cited that the two presidential finalists elected to be interviewed in the presence of each other. The finalists were asked a battery of questions about their leadership styles, vision vis-a-vis the Colegio and other insightful questions. The staff's memo was brought up during the interview session. One candidate commented, "If I were president, I would view the staff's conduct as gross insubordination."[60] The other commented, "[I am] incensed for the board's sake; that staff memo reflects negatively on the board and jeopardizes [the] interview process."[61] Years later, Jose Angel Gutierrez commented that he and the other finalist had agreed that in the event one of them got the job, the other would serve as his assistant.[62]

Shortly after the candidate interviews, the Board of Trustees scheduled a three day retreat. By this time a clear division was evident in the Board of Trustees. The eleven member board was evenly split with five members opposing and five members supporting the search. The board's chair represented the critical swing vote.

The Board of Trustees held its retreat on October 3–5, 1980. Only six board members attended the retreat. Those present constituted the board's chair and five members who opposed the presidential search. The board retreat enabled the consensus represented to solidify their power base.

The Board of Trustees (six out of eleven) reached agreement on several issues during the retreat. They determined that the process utilized in the presidential search had not complied with the mandate of the board and therefore decided to establish a new Presidential Search Committee to be chaired by the board's chair. They determined that the presidency would not be filled until after the NWASC accreditation review and that the board had no reason to discontinue the acting presidency of Irma Gonzales unless that status would prove an obstacle to obtaining full accreditation.[63] A letter was drafted and sent to the presidential finalists, informing them that the presidential search would be deferred until a future date. Their application files would remain active.

The decisions reached during the retreat set the stage for an intense board struggle. On October 22, 1980, board members not present at the retreat served the board's chair with a formal petition for a special board meeting to be held on October 29, 1980, at Colegio Cesar Chavez.

The special board meeting of October 29, 1980 focused on several issues. First, the petitioning board members went on record indicating their disapproval of the chair's abrupt changing the meeting site from Mt. Angel to Portland. A petitioning board member stated that the abrupt change "precluded an open meeting for individuals who may have wanted to participate or come and hear."[64] The same board member also indicated his concern that one of the petitioning board members did not get the change of site message because of its abruptness.

Second, the petitioning board members questioned the legality of decisions made at the board retreat since there was no agenda or notice of a board's business meeting at the retreat. The petitioning board members felt that the decisions made at the retreat regarding the presidency constituted an illegal board business. Third, they questioned the role of Irma Gonzales as a voting board member while serving as Acting President. Fourth, they questioned the disposition of the issues relating to the presidency for Colegio.

The board minutes of October 29, 1980 revealed that the board had come upon an impasse on critical issues because of board division. This division was reinforced by one member's comment, "I think we have reached a consensus. You guys reached your consensus, we've reached our consensus."[65]

Additionally, the board members not present at the retreat had lost confidence in the board's chair. One member's comments directed at the Chair substantiated this loss of confidence. "You have acted in a very unprofessional manner in dealing with this [October 29th] meeting."[66] A second comment indicated the extent of this loss of confidence. "Uh, I, uh, personally feel that [you], again, you've fucked up, [you] fucked up because the purpose of the retreat was not to deal with the presidential search. The purpose of the retreat was specifically for training the board. You again, used the authority that we have given you to manipulate, for whatever reason and purposes."[67]

The board had become inoperable as a decision making unit. The dissenting board members had not only lost confidence in the board's chair but had also requested the removal of the Acting President. The special board meeting ended in the midst of dissension and the petitioning board members requesting a legal opinion on various issues raised in the meeting. The board chair had further frustrated the opposing board members by using parliamentary maneuvers.

The internal conflict arising from the presidential search began to transcend Colegio's institutional walls. In early 1981, individuals from the Chicano community began to voice dissatisfaction with Colegio's board and administration. Some of these individuals formed CC/CCC, Concerned Community for Colegio Cesar Chavez. The committee petitioned Colegio's board for an opportunity to voice community concerns. Among the many issues the CC/CCC raised was the cancellation of the search for a new president. The bulk of their concerns however, focused on recommendations to reorganize Colegio to afford open community participation.[68]

The CC/CCC was only one of several community entities formed to reorganize Colegio. Former staff, students and board members formed the Committee to Rebuild Colegio Cesar Chavez. The Committee to Rebuild Colegio Cesar Chavez charged Colegio with firing staff members without due process, failing to hold public meetings, continuing mismanagement, and allowing conflicts of interest on the Board of Trustees.[69] Other local Chicano organizations such as Centro Chicano Cultural and Mujeres de Oregon also expressed community concerns. The Colegio board minutes during this period revealed the extent of board division when one of the petitioning board members who had been a founder of Colegio was accused by the acting president who also served as a board member, as collaborating with the community dissenters. Colegio's failure to scan the environment and consider the sentiments of the Chicano community placed Colegio in a reactive posture regarding Colegio-Chicano community relations. The chair reacted by setting up a Colegio community forum committee to respond to community concerns. But Colegio's indifference to the community it was founded to serve had alienated a growing number of Chicano community members. The community forum came too late to placate the community opposition to Colegio's leadership.

In June, 1981, the Northwest Association of Schools and Colleges unanimously voted to deny accreditation to Colegio. It is interesting to note that one area of deficiency cited by the NWASC was the presidential search.[70] Resolution of the board's division and stabilization of Colegio's presidency came during 1981, but after accreditation review. The tenures of the board members who wanted to continue with the external search for a president expired and the board confirmed Irma Gonzales as President of Colegio on October 15, 1981.

Jose Angel Gutierrez (1998) commented that he felt that the issue of the presidency had been rigged by Irma Gonzales, citing that she had not even formally applied nor been interviewed like the other finalists. He further added that perhaps Colegio or Irma Gonzales should have been sued for the outcome of the presidential search.[71] Board minutes do reveal that Irma Gonzales did express interested in the presidency during the period of the presidential search. It is certainly interesting to note that Irma Gonzales retained her position as a voting board member while serving as acting president. She supported the opposition to continuation of the presidential search while reaffirming her interest in Colegio's presidency eventhough she had not formally applied.

ENROLLMENT

Whereas Colegio's political infighting was most evident in the second phase of Colegio's life, 1978–1983, Colegio's low student enrollment was a constant concern. Depressed student enrollments hampered Colegio Cesar Chavez's struggle to become a viable Chicano institution of higher education. Colegio's early plans projected full time enrollment levels at 350 by 1983.[72] These hopes never materialized (see Fig. 2).

It would be erroneous to conclude that Colegio's low enrollments were attributed to an insufficient student pool, the absence of a need for a Chicano college, the lack of educational interest by Chicanos, or the adequacy of mainstream higher educational institutions serving the Chicano community. Colegio's low enrollments were attributable to other causes.

First, the Colegio and HUD struggle between 1974 and 1978 had an effect on Colegio's enrollments. Jose Romero, former Director of Academic Affairs reported to the *Statesman Journal* (Salem, Oregon):

> The publicity of eviction is affecting the continued enrollment of some students and the enrollment of new students. HUD has made an impact. Everywhere we go we are told by others that they heard Colegio is closing. They ask what is going to happen.[73]

HUD's indecisive behavior convinced Colegio leaders that a "bureaucratic slowdown" had affected Colegio's chance of survival.

Second, Colegio's legal battle with NWASC compounded Colegio's instability. When the NWASC withdrew Colegio's

Figure 2: Student Enrollment

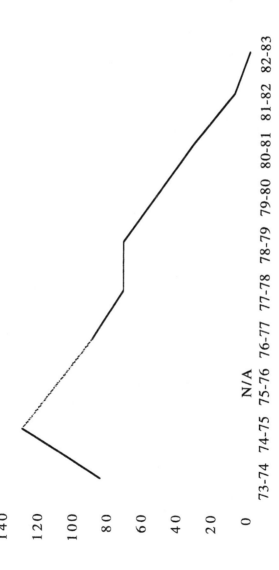

Note: Colegio's enrollments between 1973 to 1983 were compiled from various sources, including Colegio's Institutional Self Study submitted to NWASC, 1981; the *Oregonian* (Portland, Oregon), October 25, 1981; a report issued by the United States General Accounting Office, 1982; and Jose Romero's Chronological History of Colegio, no date.

accreditation candidacy in 1977, Colegio reported that summer classes had to be canceled due to loss of accreditation. The momentary loss of accreditation also affected Colegio's recruitment efforts.

Third, some segments of the Chicano community viewed Colegio's College Without Walls educational structure as inferior to traditional notions of what a college education was "supposed to be." Based on this assumption, some dismissed any possibility of attending Colegio.

Fourth, political infighting and internal deficiencies undermined Colegio's public image. Erosion of institutional credibility, particularly after 1978 took its toll. Whether the basis for the erosion was substantiated or not, the effect was the same. It created impediments towards recruitment. A former Colegio recruiter noted that students were told that Colegio acknowledged past shortcomings and that Colegio's leadership was committed to correcting past shortcomings and to progress. The recruiter noted that the erosion of public confidence served as a difficult obstacle towards recruitment. Shortly after loss of accreditation candidacy, the recruiter became disillusioned and left Colegio.

Fifth, during Colegio's ten year history, the school had only two official recruiters. Colegio depended heavily on the unofficial recruiting efforts of its students, staff, and board members to supplement the school's recruiting efforts. It was a significant, yet insurmountable shortcoming on Colegio's part not to invest substantial funds in a recruitment effort.

Sixth, on several occasions, Colegio's board minutes disclosed that financial aid awards were inadequate to support a student attending Colegio. Inadequate financial packages discouraged students from enrolling. Seventh, Colegio's educational program was not designed to attract traditional college bound high school graduates. Colegio's educational program aimed to serve an older student populace who did not require a traditional learning environment and who could learn independently. Thus, Colegio lost out on a potential student pool. Eighth, Colegio's physical plant, particularly the inoperable heating system between 1975–1980, contributed to some students' decision to leave or not attend Colegio.

Collectively, these and other factors served to constrain Colegio's efforts to develop a substantial student body and thereby strengthen Colegio's viability. Colegio also needed effective leadership to increase its viability.

LEADERSHIP

The caliber of an organization's leadership influences an organization's success. Leadership in institutions of higher education includes administration and the Board of Trustees. Effective leadership and management in an organization in crisis is a complex and multidimensional challenge. Colegio Cesar Chavez faced significant survival issues which required able leadership from the President and Board of Trustees.

Studying Colegio's leadership, one easily observes strong commitment and diligence to establish and develop a viable Chicano college. However, shortcomings in leadership resources, from Colegio's President to the Board of Trustees, undermined this commitment and diligence.

President

As discussed earlier, the significant turnover in Colegio's presidency, a total of four presidents between 1973 and 1983, precluded continuity and stability thereby undermining effective institutional leadership.

Compounding this dilemma was that only one of Colegio's presidents had professional management experience in higher education. This particular individual's management experience was limited to middle management. Although the majority of Colegio's presidents had masters degrees, only one had an academic background in education (B.A.).

The dearth of academic and management experience in higher education, and lack of presidential continuity point to serious shortcomings in Colegio's presidency. Colegio, an organization in crisis, required leadership that understood how organizations, particularly educational organizations functioned; had academic or professional management experience including budget and policy making in higher education; and had ample tenure to develop and implement strategies to address complex problems confronting Colegio. Colegio's institutional stability, lack of a fiscal base, and the limited pool of Chicano professionals in higher education administration acted as obstacles to Colegio securing top administrators.

Board of Trustees

Colegio's leadership from the Board of Trustees was also less than optimal. Colegio's board did not have sufficient diversity. As John Nason, an authority on trusteeships commented, "A truly effective board is likely to be composed of individuals who bring diverse experience, talents and attitudes to the resolution of institutional problems."[74] Besides experiencing significant turnover in membership, Colegio's Board of Trustees lacked diversity, thus undermining its effectiveness and leadership.

An incomplete board undermined the diversity of Colegio's board. Colegio's bylaws called for a thirteen member board. Colegio's Board of Trustees operated the majority of the time with nine or ten board members two of which were faculty and student representatives. In addition, from 1979 until Colegio's closure in 1983, the president was also a voting board member. In sum, the board vacancies and internal representatives (faculty, student and President) reduced external representation.

In addition, the constitution of the board lacked representatives from several areas. For instance, Colegio did not adequately tap into the business sector. During the early years, two businessmen who served on the Mt. Angel College board continued their trusteeship into Colegio, yet their tenures were short. Colegio had only one businessman, (owner of an advertising and public relations firm) with a sustained tenure. Business leaders could have provided useful business advice and might have acted as intermediates in financial relationship contacts, both of which Colegio greatly needed.

Colegio's Board of Trustees also generally lacked representation from the academic community external of Colegio. This representation would have greatly aided Colegio by informally linking with other area higher educational institutions and gaining additional academic insights to institutional issues.

Representation from the political community (community, county, state) was nonexistent. Additionally, Colegio's Board of Trustees lacked ethnic diversity. During the early years, several non-minority individuals served short tenures as board members. However, between 1973–1983, only one non-minority individual served a sustained tenure.

Colegio's Board of Trustees could have been greatly upgraded by increasing its diversity. This diversity would have been beneficial in augmenting Colegio's credibility and professional expertise, and serving as a significant fund raising corps. Diversity would have increased Colegio's effectiveness and thus leadership from the Board of Directors. Strong leadership was necessary to carry Colegio through its crises and to establish it as a viable non-traditional institution.

A NON-TRADITIONAL INSTITUTION

Colegio's institutional feature of being a Chicano experimental college had its strengths and weaknesses. On one side, Colegio's emphasis on Chicano self-determination and commitment towards an experimental academic structure gave Colegio its special institutional character. On the opposite side, Colegio's Chicano and experimental character placed Colegio in the position of an outsider in the social and educational environments.

This notion of Colegio being an outsider can first be viewed in the context of Colegio's "sense of community." Colegio drew much of its supporters outside the boundaries of the City of Mt. Angel. An informal inimical relationship existed between the community of Mt. Angel and Colegio. An *Oregon Statesman* editorial cited, "the people of Mt. Angel have themselves demonstrated scant interest in understanding or helping the struggling college. Colegio has been treated like a tumor in the body of the community."[75] A reporter commented that the community saw Colegio as a glorified grade school. This context placed Colegio Cesar Chavez as an outsider in the community of Mt. Angel.

Colegio's unique Chicano and experimental character also created difficulties for the NWASC. As most NWASC member schools and NWASC commissioners were involved in traditional educational models, Colegio Cesar Chavez's Chicano and experimental synthesis did not fit the NWASC's norm. Two NWASC individuals assigned the task of producing a NWASC evaluation of Colegio cited their uneasiness. "Colegio Cesar Chavez constitutes a unique institutional setting which poses great difficulty for a visiting team in arriving at an evaluative judgment."[76]

Realizing this, Colegio's leadership took great efforts to try to sensitize NWASC to Colegio's unique circumstances. Colegio's leaders pondered NWASC's institutional evaluation procedures. They raised questions such as, do evaluations that focus on procedures used to evaluate mainstream institutions adequately and equitably evaluate a fledgling innovative institution like Colegio? It is in this sense that

Colegio's Chicano and experimental synthesis served as a challenge to NWASC's traditional educational and evaluation models.

While the NWASC evaluators acknowledged difficulty in evaluating Colegio, others believed that the burden lay not on the evaluators but on the institution. For instance, while Colegio had been allotted federal funds, HEW deferred its decision to release student financial aid money until a government sponsored evaluation team visited Colegio and investigated Colegio's progress toward accreditation. Release of student financial aid funds depended on a positive determination. The government evaluation was negative. The evaluators further commented: "If the Colegio determined to be entirely experimental we argued, a more substantial burden rested upon them to spell out their educational objective than would be true of another institution."[77] The words "more substantial burden" exposed the consultants' views that educational objectives, and/or educational evaluations of experimental colleges need to be more explicit than those afforded or expected of traditional institutions.

This attitude was not restricted to Colegio, but rather was pervasive among critics of experimental learning. As Gilbert Roman, Chicano author, stated:

> Problems which are unique to alternative education are problems of simple survival. Surviving in a traditional system and competing against the system. System people such as federal, state and local educational units are snobbish, cliquish and educational elitists.[78]

The author further added, "It would be potentially and blatantly a lie to portend that Chicano alternative programs in higher education have gained tremendous acceptance in all circles.[79]

These three illustrations indicate how Colegio Cesar Chavez's Chicano and experimental synthesis served to make Colegio a non-traditional institution amidst a traditional social and educational community. Adverse national trends affecting general higher education further compounded Colegio's non-traditional stance.

NATIONAL TRENDS

Significant national trends amplified Colegio's institutional problems. The national trends included a shrinking market share of private higher education; an economic recession triggering retrenchment in higher education; a decrease in federal funding to higher education; a growing trend of social conservatism overshadowing notions of democratic ideals of the 1960s; and a significant decrease of political activism within the Chicano community after the mid 1970s.

Shrinking Market

America's private higher education has not retained the vigor and dominance it once held. The adjectives vigor and dominance have been replaced by constriction. "While private colleges and universities accounted for 66 percent of the institutions in 1950, by 1975 this figure had fallen to 52 percent."[80] Constriction of private higher education was also evident in student enrollments. Between 1950 and 1976, private higher education's "percentage of the total [student pool] dropped from 50 to 24 percent."[81]

Much of this constriction can be related to three factors. First was the expansion of public higher education following World War II. This expansion afforded more individuals an opportunity to attend college. The community college sector expanded the fastest, more than doubling after 1955. The federal government reinforced the expansion of public education through the G.I. Bill in 1944 and other efforts of the 1960s.

Second, demographic trends evident in the 1970s led to further restrictions in higher education. Many educational journals in higher education focused on declining student enrollment. David Breneman's *The College Enrollment Crisis: What Every Trustee Must Know* (1978), is an excellent reference on declining enrollments during 1970s. As indicated by Breneman and a host of other writers, the pool of traditional college age students leveled off in 1975 and was projected to steadily decline well into the 1990s. Since the average private campus is smaller than public institutions, private institutions will feel the enrollment decline more quickly. "Ninety percent have enrollments under 2,500."[82]

Third, private higher education has been traditionally more expensive than its public counterpart. Tuition rates have been a major reason for cost disparity. "Private tuition was 2.4 times higher than public tuition in 1956–1967 and that ratio jumped to 4.8 times higher in 1975–76."[83] This tuition gap contributed to the constriction of private higher education, particularly during poor economic times as was the case during the early 1980s.

Retrenchment in Higher Education

Higher education's growth experienced during the post war year slowed
down during the late 1970s and 1980s. Shrinking resources for higher
education became the norm during this period. Decline in higher
education can be traced to various things including shrinking of the
traditional college age pool, reduced federal funding, inflation, and a
generally poor economy. K.P. Mortimer and M.L. Tierney's *The Three
"Rs" of the Eighties: Reduction, Reallocation and Retrenchment*
(1979), carries an appropriate title for the challenges which faced
higher education during these years.

Many institutions focused on strategies to raise more revenue;
reduce expenditures by trimming programs and part-time personnel;
reallocate institutional funds; employ marketing efforts to attract more
traditional age students; and tap other student pools such as the adult
learner. Responding to fiscal retrenchment, the State University of New
York at Albany, in an elaborate process, terminated twenty-six degree
programs and several academic units. The move was to generate a pool
of resources to allocate to programs with greater need and priority.
Besides internal policies, institutions implemented external policies,
encouraging inter-institutional cooperation. Some higher educational
cooperation such as combined academic programs to either strengthen a
said program or to share resources had proven useful. The Oregon State
University and Western Oregon University's merger of education
departments in 1983 was an excellent example of inter-institutional
cooperation. Other forms such as regional or statewide consortia also
enhanced cooperative ventures. Author F. E. Crossland recommended
inter-institutional cooperation:

> What is needed is a degree of inter-institutional cooperation, far
> exceeding anything we have known in recent years. Rather than
> fighting among ourselves, we should forthrightly identify what we
> each do best, reduce pointless duplication and redundancies, share
> resources and work together.[84]

Changes in Federal Funding

Changes in federal funding of higher education forced the development
of new leadership and management abilities to address new challenges,
yet maintain quality and service. Historically, the federal government

has played a significant role in financing post secondary education in the U.S.

This role has been premised on grounds of national security and equal opportunity and resulted in a federalization of education. During the 1980s, President Reagan opted to initiate a "new federalism." Reagan's "new federalism" aimed at reordering federal, state and local responsibilities which according to his views had become entangled in past decades. Whereas Reagan argued that the "new federalism" empowered state governments, detractors viewed it as an outright rejection of a federal responsibility for social needs including education.

In higher education, Reagan's "new federalism" would mean a change in the federal government's role in student financial aid. By the mid 1980s, federal student aid had leveled off. Grant support dropped and loan eligibility and subsidies were cut back. According to authors Edward P. St. John and Charles Byce in 1980, "all federal programs excluding GSL [had been] cut substantially."[85]

Starting during the Reagan years, the composition of federal student aid experienced a dramatic shift. This shift has continued into the 1990s. The shift has resulted in a decline in federal grant funding and a significant rise in federal student loans. This shift has likewise undermined the original intent of federal higher educational funding to enhance equal opportunity to low income students, particularly underrepresented students.

Changes in federal student aid has impinged upon equity issues such as access, choice and student retention. Efforts to cut student aid during the Reagan years did not go unchallenged. An interesting organization which formed to decry changes in federal funding was Action: Committee for Higher Education. This organization served as a national clearinghouse on student aid information. Additionally, the organization informally lobbied student aid issues. Action's membership included a long list of national educational organizations such as the American Association of Higher Education, the American Council on Education, the National Association of State Universities and Land Grant Colleges, and others. Action focused on preserving a balanced and effective student aid program. Reagan's "new federalism" was symbolic of the changing national mood towards conservatism.

Social Ideals Overshadowed

A lessened social consciousness of the 1980s and 1990s eclipsed the social ferment dominant in the 1960s and early 1970s. A number of publications have focused on this changing national mood. While Faustine Jones's, *The Changing Mood In America: Eroding Commitment* (1977), spoke to wide social issues, others like Stephen H. Adolph's, *Equality Postponed* (1984), focused on this changing mood's implication on education. Adolph pointed to the undermining of the progression of educational opportunity in higher education, particularly for minorities. The Bakke court case was symbolic of the changing mood during the late 1970s and 1980s. In the 1990s, the attacks on affirmative action in California, Texas, and Washington state continued the shift in popular thought regarding issues of equity.

Decline of the Chicano Movement

The Chicano Movement began to dissipate by the mid 1970s. This dissipation came not because social needs of the Chicano community had been fulfilled, rather because several socio-political forces undermined the progression of Chicano activism.

First, the Chicano Movement, like many other social movements had many ideologies, leaders, agendas and strategies. No single over-encompassing platform existed. The absence of a set national agenda contributed to a diffusion of energies.[86]

Second, the Chicano Movement, though independent of other interest groups (Blacks, Native Americans, etc.), became empowered by the general civil rights movement and social unrest of the 1960s and early 1970s. A shift in the national social mood away from liberal politics by the mid 1970s to a more conservative social mindset which became dominant in the 1980s undermined the climate for social political change pursued by Chicanos and other ethnic minority groups.

Third, by the mid 1970s, the Chicano leadership of Tijerina, Gutierrez, Gonzales and Cesar Chavez which had sparked Chicano activism in earlier years had peaked. Tijerina disappeared from the Chicano activism landscape (Muñoz 1989), Jose Angel Gutierrez and La Raza Unida became mired by internal divisions and defections (Navarro 1998), "Corky" Gonzales and the Crusade for Justice lost much grassroots support, became isolated, financially strapped, and retracted to Denver, Colorado (Vigil 1999) and the political impact of Cesar Chavez and the farmworker movement became lessened. Jose

Angel Gutierrez (1998) succinctly stated this changing reality regarding Chicano Movement leadership when stating "The Four Horsemen of the Chicano Movement--Cesar Chavez, Reies Lopez Tijerina, Rodolfo "Corky" Gonzales, and I--were eclipsed..."[87] The waning Chicano leadership negatively impacted the level of Chicano activism.

Fourth, by the late 1970s and 1980s, an "Hispanic" orientation and leadership began to emerge. The 1980s became coined as the "Hispanic" decade. "Hispanic," not "Chicano," was the organizational banner of emerging groups. This emerging "Hispanic" orientation promoted an accommodation and assimilationist stance in sharp contrast to the Chicano politics of protest of the 1960s and early 1970s.

Fifth, Chicano student activism and Chicano Studies in colleges and universities likewise was negatively affected during the late 1970s and 1980s. During the 1960s and early 1970s, Chicano students had been in the vanguard of Chicano activism on and off campus. Some Raza students began to gravitate to career focused student organizations, "Hispanic" fraternities, and other mainstream apolitical student organizations. The monopoly which MECHA had among Raza students on campus has been lessened. Likewise, Chicano Studies initiatives since the mid 1970s have had to struggle against cutbacks affecting the number and size of Chicano Studies programs across the U.S. Both MECHA and Chicano Studies have historically advocated in keeping the Chicano agenda in the forefront. The diminished ability of MECHA and Chicano Studies on colleges and universities to move the Chicano agenda in the last two decades has negatively affected Chicano activism (Acuña 1988).

And sixth, active federal and state repression through political surveillance and legal harassment of Chicano organizations and activists undermined Chicano activism. Law enforcement created divisions among activists. The police arrested and carried out violence against Chicano activists. Infiltration of Chicano organizations by police informants and other state sponsored tactics were also utilized. Collectively, these efforts were aimed at discrediting and undermining Chicano activism (Muñoz 1989, Gutierrez 1998, Vigil 1999).

SUMMARY

Colegio's Board Chairman, Jose Garcia said accurately and succinctly that there were "too many issues converging on Colegio."[88] Institutional and external issues continually bombarded Colegio's health and viability. Institutional issues such as Colegio's lack of a firm fiscal base adversely affected almost every facet of institutional activity. Colegio's institutional legal battles over federal foreclosure and accreditation sapped Colegio's meager fiscal and personnel resources. Institutional infighting mired Colegio's leadership, hampering critically needed progress. In addition, Colegio's declining enrollment between 1973 and 1983 was indicative of institutional deterioration rather than progress.

External issues and national trends added to Colegio's viability. Adverse national trends impinging on higher education from the mid-1970s onward created an unsupportive social context that further undermined Colegio's chances of survival. Colegio Cesar Chavez's closure in 1983 confirmed the fading dreams and hopes of Chicanos supportive of an innovative higher educational experiment--Colegio Cesar Chavez.

NOTES

1. "Ailing Colegio Endures Many Death Scenes," *Oregon Journal*, 12 October 1981, p. 7.

2. "Mondor Resigning MAC President," *Silverton Appeal-Tribune*, 18 October 1973, p. 1.

3. Interview with Jose Romero, Marion Educational Service District, Salem, Oregon, 14 April 1986.

4. Colegio Cesar Chavez, "Application and Proposal for Federal Support Under Title III, Basic Institutional Development Program," 26 April 1978, p. 8.

5. "Festivities to Begin Tonight," *Oregon Statesman*, 12 December 1979, p. 1B.

6. Susan T. Hill, *The Traditionally Black Institutions of Higher Education: 1860 to 1982*, (Washington, D.C., National Center for Education Statistics, Department of Education: U.S. Government Printing Office, 1984), p. 71.

7. Interview with Celedonio "Sonny" Montez, Inter-face Inc., Portland, Oregon, 18 April 1986.

8. "Its Worst Crisis Over, Chicano College Forges Ahead," *Oregonian*, 17 February 1980, p. D15.

9. Interview with Robin Aaberg, Ms. Aaberg's home, Hillsboro, Oregon, 7 April 1986.

10. "Colegio Sit-in Planned to Protest Eviction Notice," *Capital Journal*, 26 March 1975, sec. 1, p. 1.

11. Montez.

12. "Response to Colegio's Suit Delayed for Legal Advice," *Oregonian*, 20 June 1977, p. Bl.

13. Colegio Cesar Chavez v. Northwest Association of Schools and Colleges, II Crist. (U.S. District Court), 383 (1977).

14. Colegio Cesar Chavez vs. Northwest Association of Schools and Colleges, IV McCloskey. (U.S. District Court), 899 (1977).

15. "Colegio Wins Temporary Reprieve," *Oregon Statesman* 8 July 1977, p. Cl.

16. Joan Kalvelage, "Cinco Exemplos," *Edcentric* (n. d.), p. 36.

17. John Nason, *Nature of Trusteeship: The Role and Responsibilities of College and University Boards*, (Washington, D.C.: Association of Governing Boards of Universities and Colleges, 1982), p. 66.

18. Jose Romero, "Chronological History of Colegio Cesar Chavez," Personal Files of Jose Romero, Salem, Oregon, p. 2.

19. "HUD Considering Foreclosure on Mt. Angel College," *Silverton Appeal-Tribune*, 15 November 1973, p. 1.

20. Romero, "Chronological History of Colegio Cesar Chavez," p. 2.

21. "HUD Considering Foreclosure on Mt. Angel College," *Silverton Appeal-Tribune*, 15 November 1973, p. 1.

22. Romero, Interview.

23. "Colegio Officials File Discrimination Charge," *Capital Journal*, 5 June 1974, sec. 1, p. 1.

24. Romero, "Chronological History of Colegio Cesar Chavez," p. 2.

25. "HUD Talks Tough on Colegio," *Capital Journal*, 1 April 1975, sec. 1, p. 1.

26. "Colegio Officials to Confer in D.C. on Foreclosure," *Oregon Statesman*, 10 May 1975, sec. 1, p. 8.

27. Romero, "Chronological History of Colegio Cesar Chavez," p. 7.

28. "Colegio Officials are Optimistic After Meeting with HUD in D.C.," *Oregon Statesman*, 14 May 1977, sec. 1, p. 1.

29. "Colegio Ordered Off Mt. Angel Site," *Oregonian*, 3 September 1976, p. 1.

30. "75 March Through Portland Rain for Colegio Cesar Chavez," *Oregon Statesman*, 7 December 1976, p. Cl.

31. "Official Denies HUD Trying to Discourage Colegio," *Oregon Statesman*, 16 December 1976, p. A8.

32. "Colegio to HUD, Buy Your Own Set of Keys," *Oregon Statesman*, 14 January 1977, p. A2.

33. "Colegio Salutes First Graduating Class" *Oregonian*, 1 July 1977, sec. 3, p. All.

34. "Colegio Awaits Word as Eviction Nears," *Oregon Statesman*, 14 June 1977, p. A7.

35. "Evicted Colegio Demands HUD Practices be Probed," *Oregon Journal*, 21 September 1977, p. 1.

36. Montez.

37. "There is Room for Compromise in Colegio Cesar Chavez Case," *Statesman Journal-Capital Journal*, 2 October 1977, p. D3.

38. "Colegio Vows to Battle New HUD Eviction Order," *Oregon Statesman*, 3 March 1978, p. All.

39. "HUD Sells Campus to Chavez College for Quarter Million," *Oregon Statesman*, 5 July 1978, p. Al.

40. Aaberg.

41. Montez.

42. Romero, Interview.

43. Dr. Cordelia Candelaria, "Toward Securing Full Accreditation: Colegio Cesar Chavez Consultation with Dr. Cordelia Candelaria," 23 June 1980, Site Visit I.

44. Northwest Association of Schools and Colleges, "Candidate for Accreditation: Biennial Evaluation." 11 May 1978, p. 1.

45. Ibid., p. 2.

46. "Colegio Officials to Confer in D.C. on Foreclosure," *Oregon Statesman*, 10 May 1975, sec. 1, p. 8.

47. Interview with Jose Garcia, Oregon State Department of Education, Salem, Oregon, 9 April 1986.

48. "Colegio Desperately Tries to Stay Alive," *Oregon Journal*, 20 November 1976, p. 3.

49. Colegio Cesar Chavez, Press Release Concerning the Purchase of Campus, n. d., p. 2.

50. Candelaria, p. 6.

51. Ibid.

52. Montez.

53. Garcia.

54. Colegio Cesar Chavez, "Transcription of Tape Recording of Termination Hearing," 5 June 1980, p. 4.

55. Colegio Cesar Chavez, Mt. Angel, Oregon, Board of Trustees Minutes, Meeting of 23 September 1980.

56. Colegio Cesar Chavez, Mt. Angel, Oregon, Board of Trustees Minutes, Meeting of 20 June 1980.

57. Colegio Cesar Chavez, Mt. Angel, Oregon, Board of Trustees Minutes, Meeting of 10 September 1980.

58. Colegio Cesar Chavez, Mt. Angel, Oregon, Board of Trustees Minutes, Meeting of 27 June 1981.

59. Staff of Colegio Cesar Chavez, Staff Memo to Final Presidential Candidates, 1 October 1980.

60. Colegio Cesar Chavez, Mt. Angel, Oregon, Board of Trustees Minutes, Presidential Candidate Interviews, 1 October 1980, p. 5.

61. Ibid.

62. Jose Angel Gutierrez, *The Making of a Militant: Lessons From Cristal*, (Madison, University of Wisconsin, 1998), p. 274.

63. Colegio Cesar Chavez, "Report of the Chair on the Consensus of the Board at Retreat: Regarding the Presidential Search," 29 October 1980.

64. Colegio Cesar Chavez, Mt. Angel, Oregon, Board of Trustees Minutes, Special Meeting of 29 October 1980.

65. Ibid.

66. Ibid.

67. Ibid.

68. Concerned Community for Colegio Cesar Chavez, "Agenda of Concerns," 26 March 1981.

69. "Accreditation Goal for Struggling Colegio Cesar Chavez," *Oregonian*, 16 March 1981, p. Bl.

70. Colegio Cesar Chavez, Mt. Angel, Oregon, Board of Trustees Minutes, Meeting of 27 June 1980.

71. Gutierrez, p.274.

72. Colegio Cesar Chavez, "Application and Proposal for Federal Support Under Title III, Basic Institutional Development Program," 26 April 1978.

73. "Colegio Staff Believes Future Looks Bright," *Oregon Statesman*, 18 October 1975, sec. 2, p. 18.

74. John Nason, *Nature of Trusteeship: The Role and Responsibilities of College and University Boards*, (Washington, D.C.: Association of Governing Boards of Universities and Colleges, 1982), p. 67.

75. "Colegio's Aims are Valid Despite Financial Plight," *Oregon Statesman*, 30 August 1976, p. B12.

76. Northwest Association of Schools and Colleges, "Candidate for Accreditation: Biennial Evaluation," 11 May 1978, p. 1.

77. William W. Jellema and William A. Hunter, Consultants to the Department of Health, Education, and Welfare, "Report to the Director of Accreditation and Institutional Eligibility Staff: Department of Health,

Education and Welfare; Office of Education, Bureau of Postsecondary Education Concerning Colegio Cesar Chavez," 30 April 1975, p. 7.

78. Gilbert D. Roman, "Chicano Alternatives in Higher Education" in *Chicanos in Higher Education*, ed. Henry J. Casso and Gilbert D. Roman (New Mexico: University of New Mexico Press, 1976), p. 175.

79. Ibid.

80. David W. Breneman and Chester E. Finn, Jr., ed., *An Uncertain Future* (Washington, D.C.: Brookings Institute, 1978), p. 19.

81. Ibid.

82. Ibid., p. 218.

83. Ibid., p. 27.

84. F. E. Crossland, "Learning to Cope with a Downward Slope," *Change* (July-August 1980), p. 18.

85. Edward P. St. John and Charles Byce, "The Changing Federal Role in Student Financial Aid," *New Directions for Higher Education*, no. 40 (1980), p. 30.

86. Avelardo Valdez, "Selective Determinants in Maintaining Social Movement Organizations: Three Case Studies From the Chicano Community," (n.p., n.d.), p. 30.

87. Gutierrez, p. 290.

88. Garcia.

CHAPTER 6

Conclusions and Insights for Chicano College Promoters

Seek what you are capable of, and be capable of what you seek.

Leonardo da Vinci[1]

The preceding analysis of Colegio Cesar Chavez's demise raises some nagging questions. Was Colegio Cesar Chavez doomed to fail? Judging from Colegio and other Chicano alternative educational institutional closures, can the conclusion be made that Chicano educational institutions are anachronistic? If not, what are some insights that can be gleaned from Colegio's closure to aid future promoters of Chicano colleges? These are the guiding questions for the following narrative.

CONCLUSION: "WAS COLEGIO DOOMED TO FAIL?"

I posed the question, "Was Colegio doomed to fail?" to individuals formerly associated with Colegio Cesar Chavez. A former Chair of Colegio's Board commented:

> After we got the campus, I remembered Patricia Harris, [HUD Secretary], when she came out to hand us the title to Colegio, I'll never forget her, she said, "Why do you people want to start a college? Other colleges are failing. Why do you want a college? You could start a business, a housing project, anything but a college." I will always remember that because it was true. The colleges were losing students like crazy and here we were trying to get a colegio

started. We took a white elephant really. It was doomed for failure I
guess from the very beginning. We had too many problems in starting
a college. We didn't have the money to implement programs on site.
Too many undertakings and not enough money.[2]

When I asked Colegio's former Dean of Academics what it would
have taken to have Colegio exist today, he responded, "Had we had
manna from heaven."[3] He further added that the fiscal base was a
central institutional need. Two evaluators from the regional accrediting
agency cited in a 1978 report to NWASC, "There are so many "ifs"
crucial to the Colegio's future: grants, funding, resolution of legal
problems, retaining the campus, etc."[4]

Those comments and substantiating evidence led me to conclude
that Colegio was doomed to fail. It faced overwhelming odds in
obtaining institutional stability, establishing a fiscal base, securing a
vibrant student enrollment, struggling with legal battles with HUD and
NWASC; and obtaining full accreditation. It also faced developmental
challenges of establishing an experimental academic model, developing
academic programs, establishing fiscal and management systems, and
deploying a network of student services (counseling, etc.). Colegio
faced the need to upgrade the poor conditions of its physical plant,
reverse a significant erosion of its public image among the Chicano and
non-Chicano community, and other fundamental undertakings involved
in founding and developing an institution of higher education.
Compounding those immense challenges were the stark realities of a
shrinking market share of private higher education; an economic
recession triggering retrenchment in higher education, decrease in
federal funding to higher education; a growing trend of social
conservatism overshadowing notions of social democratic ideals of the
60s, and a significant decrease of activism within the Chicano
community after the mid 1970s.

Indeed, Colegio faced significant external and institutional
challenges. The challenges generated a multiplicity of issues
converging on a small, private Chicano college that lay outside
mainstream higher education and outside the Chicano population
concentrations of the Southwest.

Colegio Cesar Chavez began at the end of the social pendulum's
swing which had given force to a collective activity including the
experimental college movement, the Chicano Movement, expanding
higher education, a robust economy, and a socially conscious national

mood. As Colegio Cesar Chavez and the rest of the country reached the mid 1970s and progressed toward the 1980s, the backward swing of the social pendulum began to exert its effect. This emerging social milieu and Colegio's institutional problems precluded the nurturing and rooting of an institution--Colegio Cesar Chavez.

Colegio Cesar Chavez did not cease to exist because it represented an obsolete or anachronistic premise. On the contrary, Chicano, Black, Native American, and women's colleges have contributed to a diversity in higher education which enhance equal educational opportunity. In addition, these institutions have contributed by producing leadership which steadfastly advocates reform to make higher education pluralistic in all facets of the campus. To argue that these institutions are anachronistic is to propose that a pluralistic system of higher education is already in place or not necessary. To do so would ignore the obvious reality of educationally impoverished minority communities, women, and older non-traditional students.

Concluding that Chicano and other minority institutions are not anachronistic, what insights can Colegio's closure extend to future promoters of Chicano higher educational institutions?

INSIGHTS TO FUTURE PROMOTERS

Dilemmas facing higher education are numerous. The economic, educational, social, and political forces impinging on higher education are substantial and preclude simple remedies. The individuality and internal events taking place at each institution compound these impinging forces. Articles such as "A Survival Kit for Invisible Colleges" and "Survival Gear for Small Colleges" imply that the application of an X formula will consequently restore institutional health or preclude demise. There does not exist however, any prototype scheme guaranteeing institutional health and vigor in America's more than 4,457 degree granting private and public colleges and universities.[5] The following narrative does not divulge any dramatic insights to future promoters of Chicano colleges. What can be said is that some insights do exist that can lead promoters of Chicano colleges to develop more sophisticated Chicano higher educational institutions. The following are some insights into leadership, preliminary planning, fiscal base, educational niche, historical evolution, local and national scanning, political action, and others.

Leadership

Board of Trustees

Institutional leadership is a critical key influencing the success and quality of a higher educational institution. A college's board of trustees is an integral component of that leadership. As John W. Nason commented, "The decisions they make and the manner in which they implement policy determines not only the daily operation of a college, but also its future."[6] Adding to this, J. D. Millett, in *Mergers and Closures in Higher Education: Ten Case Studies* (1976), pointed out that colleges forced to close share several features. Among them was ineffective leadership from the board of trustees.

The literature on trusteeship and Colegio's experience indicate that an effective board has several requirements. First, the board must be diverse, thus bringing varying perspectives and resources to specific institutional concerns. Second, the board must be sufficiently large, since private colleges depend heavily on raising money from private sources. This logically dictates a large board composed of generous donors and individuals prepared to participate in fund raising efforts. According to John W. Nason, the average private board consists of twenty-six members.

Third, exiting administrators should not be invited to sit on the board. Perhaps an advisory board position would be more appropriate. Fourth, college administrators, whether acting or permanent, should not be a voting part of the board. Fifth, neither an institution's faculty nor students should serve on the board. If such a service is crucial, an advisory faculty and student committee or faculty and student representation from another institution could fulfill the need.

Sixth, continuity of individual board tenure affording stability of board leadership by enhancing maturity of ideas, interaction, and personalities is advantageous.

Seventh, a diverse and energetic advisory unit supplements a standing board with expertise, contacts, and influence useful for networking, marketing, and fund raising. Eighth, individuals from external institutions of higher education (administrators, board members, etc.) should be recruited to serve on the board to provide insights in operating an institution of higher education. The board of trustees is the primary source of institutional leadership. This leadership is responsible for the direction of the institution and mandates given to the college president.

President

A college president is hired by the board of trustees to implement board policy. A college presidency requires an individual with optimal experience, commitment, and ability to direct a higher educational institution. Such a prerequisite calls for a college's monetary investment and critical selection. J. D. Millett (1976) emphasized that inadequate administrative leadership contributes to college closures. An incapable administrator undermines efforts to establish and develop a college in both immediate and extended operations.

Institutional leadership from the board of trustees and the president is a driving force contributing to an institution's viability. Lacking strong leadership at either level significantly hampers any institution.

Preliminary Planning

Preliminary planning by leaders of new institutions is crucial to an institution's viability. Chicano leaders founded Colegio through sudden opportunity rather than by planned design. Chicano leaders seized an opportunity to salvage a dying institution. Future promoters of Chicano colleges will have to struggle with fundamental issues such as the feasibility of a college. Some individuals may view this as passive, lacking initiative, yet any initiative to found a college without extensive preliminary planning is shortsighted.

A feasibility assessment needs to focus on fundamental issues of available resources (fiscal and personnel), target group, location, possible academic niche, and others. I am convinced that the need for higher education exists in the Chicano community. The need is obvious, the strategy is the critical issue. Can Chicanos marshal resources to nourish a fledgling institution or should energy be aimed at gaining access to mainstream institutions?

Financial Base

A major aspect of preliminary planning should be a strategy to establish an adequate financial base. As Michael Olivas (1982) indicated, whereas many Black colleges were sponsored by religious organizations, Indian colleges by the federal government (Bureau of Indian Affairs), and women's colleges by endowments of wealthy individuals, Chicano colleges had to rely on federal largess for survival and development. Colegio's overdependence on federal funds underlines Olivas's point. This overdependence proved fatal when Colegio lost its accreditation, thus losing much needed federal monies.

Future Chicano college promoters should recognize that federal aid is a "velvet coffin," it is comfortable yet deadly. Federal money is necessary, but making it an institution's mainstay is shortsighted. Private sources need to be nurtured and expanded. Usually, private colleges heavily depend on private sources. Investment of time, personnel, and money identifying private funding is fundamental. Establishing an endowment or quasi-endowment is a basic institutional need. Specific annual fund raising and capital fund drives should be routine activities. Corporate and college partnerships serve well to supplement fiscal resources, either in form of scholarship programs or auxiliary campus programs.

It is critical that a college's leadership be directly involved in efforts to secure private monies. Additionally, a development office should be an integral part of the institution. Extensive efforts to tap private sources is necessary for all higher education institutions. In times of scarce resources, the need and competition for private monies intensifies. An institution that does not organize its efforts and resources to secure private or public funding awaits a lingering death.

An Educational Niche

Future Chicano college promoters will find it easier to establish a financial base if they can create or secure an educational niche. The business sector is keen in generating and securing a market niche. When one hears the name SONY, one immediately conjures images of electronic equipment; when one hears the name Apple, Inc., one immediately thinks of computers. There are parallels to this in the higher educational community. Some higher educational institutions pride themselves as being recognized as a premier teaching college, technology focused school, or a progressive college in the experimental tradition.

Future promoters of Chicano colleges can greatly benefit in generating an educational niche. In the case of Colegio, its unique feature of being a Chicano experimental college was excellent, yet Colegio never developed an educational niche. Had it concentrated on developing a sophisticated bilingual and bicultural program or an educational research initiative focusing on Chicanos, it could have established an excellent educational niche. It could have produced

Chicano bilingual teachers, developed bilingual and bicultural resource materials, trained non-minority teachers and administrators in cultural awareness seminars, assisted private businesses in marketing strategies to reach the rapidly growing Chicano community, and offered language or cultural classes to professionals whose work entailed the expanding Chicano or other minority communities. If future Chicano college promoters can generate or secure an educational niche, it would greatly aid a fledgling Chicano college, particularly during times of scarce financial resources.

Historical Evolution

Educational niches are often generated through an institution's tradition or evolution. Black and women's colleges had a long evolutionary history. They began as elementary institutions and evolved into preparatory schools, culminating in post-secondary institutions. Colegio and other Chicano colleges had no such historical base. In Colegio's case, a reporter succinctly stated, "Wednesday morning it was Mt. Angel College, Wednesday night it became Colegio Cesar Chavez."[7] Colegio became an instant Chicano college. Chicano leaders grasped the opportunity to be creators of their own education.

Whereas Colegio lacked a historical base, the National Hispanic University in San Jose, California evolved into a post secondary institution in 1982. Before that year, it served as BABEL, Bay Area Bilingual Educational League. BABEL was a teacher training center in bilingual education. It became highly successful and widely known. BABEL's success enabled its leaders to establish organizational roots which later contributed to reorganizing efforts to found the National Hispanic University.[8]

The benefits of a historical base as evidenced in Black and women's colleges and in particular the National Hispanic University may warrant consideration by future Chicano college promoters. Future Chicano college promoters will benefit from considering how the lack of a historical base may detract from a college's leadership, credibility, and institutional development (fiscal, personnel and programmatic.)

Local and National Scanning

Individuals developing a new institution or progressing an institution with an historical base must be cognizant of local and national issues affecting their efforts. The days when organizations viewed themselves as "self-contained entities," not burdened with external social, and political issues have long disappeared. Organizational theorists now use social system models to illustrate that organizations are indeed sub-units of a larger social system. As such, they are influenced by social, political and economic issues.

As social organizations, educational institutions exist in a fluid environment. Future Chicano college promoters should be cognizant of a changing environment. They need to continually scan the environment for forces detrimental to an institution. National trends evident during Colegio's founding (economic recession, decline in federal spending on education, shrinking of a private college market) are important to note. Chicano college promoters should assess the implications of these and other trends on the founding or development of a Chicano college.

In addition, environmental scanning needs to include the local scene. In Colegio's case, the solidifying of Chicano organizations decrying the status of Colegio placed Colegio leaders in a reactive stance. Colegio had become isolated from those it aimed to serve. Failure to scan the local community and glean useful information identifying true or perceived institutional weaknesses critically undermined Colegio's effectiveness and credibility. Consciously scanning the national and local environments enhances the feasibility of founding or developing a Chicano college.

Political Action

Developing vigorous political action will also enhance the feasibility of a fledgling Chicano college. In 1975, several state senators introduced a measure in the Oregon Senate requesting that the federal government declare Colegio as surplus property and entrust it to Oregon's Chicano community.[9] There exist several cases where a college or an educational initiative has secured its campus through the surplus property route. D.Q. University is one such case. Future Chicano college promoters should mount similar political activity on state and federal governments to focus on issues affecting Chicano higher education.

Howard University in Washington, D.C., a Black four-year private institution, has a unique relationship to the federal government. Congress makes direct annual appropriations to Howard University. Chicano leaders need to argue that such arrangements be extended to

Chicano institutions, particularly since Blacks have an established higher education network while Chicanos do not. If the Black community's need is valid, so is the Chicano's.

Chicano leaders would find it helpful to mount efforts prompting state and federal governments to make revisions in existing policies that discriminate against fledgling institutions. For example, in order for institutions to be eligible for state appropriations in Oregon, institutions must be fully accredited. A central criterion for accreditation is a sound fiscal base. But that criterion places fledgling institutions such as Chicano colleges in a "catch-22." The same case can be made for federal policies.

Chicano leaders must generate interest among federal officials to focus and sponsor legislation to assist developing ethnic institutions. For instance, the federal government in the past has directed federal agencies to target federal aid to Black colleges. The Tribally Controlled Community College Assistance Act (PL 95–471) assisted Native American institutions. In sum, these are ethnically specific efforts to aid Black and Native Americans. There exists a clear need to initiate specific efforts for Chicano/Latino institutions as well.

Chicano leaders need to consider the benefits and possibility of state-sponsored Chicano colleges. This would be most appropriate where Chicanos constitute a significant community and the state's educational record is marginal among Chicanos. The precedent for state ethnic institutions exists in the form of Grambling State University, a four-year public Black institution, and others. Granted, public Black institutions have a different history to account for their existence, yet they still exist. Why not other ethnic institutions such as Chicano colleges? Some states even sponsor public institutions that adhere to experimental models implemented at Colegio. An example is the Evergreen State College in Olympia, Washington. These are valid arguments on which Chicano college promoters can base their efforts in lobbying state and federal governments.

Additional Insights

Several additional points augment the preceding insights to Chicano college promoters. First, since past Chicano college promoters established colleges in rural areas and outside Chicano population concentrations, as well as in urban and areas of Chicano population concentrations, future promoters will benefit from studying why both settings failed. What were the transcending variables?

Second, future promoters will find it helpful to become acquainted with the literature on founding ethnic institutions, and glean what can be useful. Additionally, site visits to ethnic institutions to gather survey information useful in establishing and developing a Chicano college can prove advantageous. Of particular relevance would be Boricua College in New York, New York founded in 1974 and the National Hispanic University (NHU) in San Jose, California founded in 1981. Both institutions are still operating in 1999. How can the experience and strategy in institutional development of Boricua College and NHU be useful to Chicano college promoters? In reviewing NHU's 1998–99 brochure, the Chicanocentricism underscoring Chicano alternative educational institutions of the 1970s, is not evident. Did such absence positively impact the development and acceptance of NHU?

Third, Colegio Cesar Chavez's leadership excellently exploited the uses of organizational culture and symbols. Institutional concepts such as 'La familia," "Si, Se Puede," and even the college's name served as rallying points. During the continual HUD eviction attempts and NWASC's accreditation struggles, Colegio's leaders expressed significant commitment, resolve, and leadership to overcome overwhelming odds. Their actions served to excite supporter's commitment. National figures like Cesar Chavez also heartened Colegio's leaders and followers, encouraging them to pursue their organizational goal of securing the campus. Colegio's struggles exemplify an excellent case study and lesson to analyze organizational culture and symbols. Future Chicano college promoters need to similarly generate and exploit an organizational culture to reinforce their efforts.

Fourth, how can future Chicano college promoters benefit from examining the efforts of HACU, Hispanic Association of Colleges and Universities. Naturally, HACU's ideology and strategy would be different from that of Chicanos, yet I suspect that there exists some insights helpful to Chicano college promoters.

CONCLUDING REMARKS

Colegio Cesar Chavez's closure provides Chicano college promoters a useful case study from which to glean insights. Colegio's strengths and weaknesses can be incorporated or improved in new forms of Chicano colleges. The new forms need to be more sophisticated to absorb environmental and institutional crises and be viable higher education institutions. I do not imply that Chicanos should place their educational hopes solely on Chicano institutions. Rather, Chicanos need to continually advocate access into mainstream institutions, and supplement this opportunity with self-determining Chicano colleges and schools. Chicano need and marginality in higher education and in education in general is a given. Chicanos need to formulate strategy on how to achieve educational parity. Chicanos need to be creators of their own destiny. As the popular Chicano movement slogan states, "SI, SE PUEDE"—YES, IT CAN BE DONE!

NOTES

1. Leonardo da Vinci, cited in Elihu Carranza, *Chicanismo: Philosophical Fragment* (Dubuque, Kendall/Hunt Publishing Co., 1978), p. 13.

2. Interview with Jose Garcia, Oregon State Department of Education, Salem, Oregon, 9 April 1986.

3. Interview with Peter DeGarmo, former Academic Dean, Mr. DeGarmo's home, Portland, Oregon, 3 April 1986.

4. Northwest Association of Schools and Colleges, "Candidate for Accreditation: Biennial Evaluation," 11 May 1978, p. 2.

5. U.S. Department of Education. National Center for Education Statistics. *1997 Directory of Postsecondary Institutions*, Volume I, Degree-Granting Institutions, NCES 98–299–I. Project Officers, Samuel Barbett and Austin Lin. Washington, DC: 1998.

6. John Nason, *Nature of Trusteeship: The Role and Responsibilities of College and University Boards* Washington, D.C.: Association of Governing Boards of Universities and Colleges, 1982), p. 52.

7. "Mt. Angel Takes New Name," *Oregon Journal*, 13 December 1973, p. 2.

8. National Hispanic University, "Institutional Introductory Literature," Oakland, California, p. 1.

9. "Give Colegio to Chicanos, Measure Asks," *Oregon Statesman*, 7 May 1975, sec. 2, p. 23.

Research Tools and Methodology

SOURCES EMPLOYED IN THE STUDY

Sources used in this study include newspaper articles, interviews, public documents, institutional records and secondary published sources.

I used newspaper articles focusing on Colegio Cesar Chavez published by the *Silverton Appeal-Tribune*, (Silverton, Oregon); *Oregonian*, (Portland, Oregon); *Capital Journal*, (Salem, Oregon); and the *Statesman Journal*, (Salem, Oregon). The State of Oregon Library had indexed these newspaper articles by subject. The review of newspaper articles provided an initial source of information about Colegio Cesar Chavez. The articles were also useful in identifying issues and individuals associated with Colegio, and provided photos of historical value.

I identified and interviewed individuals associated with Colegio. These included former board members, students, faculty, administrators and community individuals. Interviews provided useful information on Colegio. These individuals supplied additional names for possible research participants.

I used several types of public documents. These included court depositions and transcripts, legal briefs and supporting documents, legal judgments, and federal agency reports focusing on Colegio Cesar Chavez. These included documents from United States General Accounting Office, the Department of Health, Education and Welfare, and the State of Oregon Department of Commerce.

It is important to note that the custodians of Colegio's institutional records declined to assist or participate in this research. Reasons for denial of access to institutional records were not presented. In speaking to one of the current board members, it was clear that Colegio's board was inactive and incomplete. Board membership amounted to three individuals. I spoke to these individuals and they were quite hesitant to speak about Colegio.

Former administrators, board members, faculty and students supplied me with excellent originals or copies of institutional records, enabling me to flesh out my institutional case study of Colegio. Included in these were board minutes, grant proposals, institutional evaluation reports by the NWASC and independent consultants, school catalogs, correspondence, photographs, faculty and board rosters, institutional self-studies, fiscal reports and audits, student lists, faculty handbook, organizational charts, etc. The individuals supplying these documents assisted me in clearing the obstacle placed by individuals having custody of Colegio's institutional records.

Secondary sources supplemented the primary data for this research. These included journals, books, and ERIC documents. The themes of these materials ranged from historical works on the experimental college movement to organizational works focusing on trusteeship in higher education. These materials served as the context and points of analysis in which to place Colegio Cesar Chavez's closure.

METHODOLOGY

This research project is a qualitative inquiry into the history of Colegio Cesar Chavez. My methodology included qualitative research procedures. The research included consulting primary and secondary sources.

Interview Guide and Distillation of Interview Data

The following procedures were used to gather and process data:
1. Research individual to be interviewed and complete interview file card.

    Name:
    Address/Phone:
    Current Occupation:
    Connection with Colegio: Years:

      Time/Place of Interview:

      Other possible sources of information:

2. Develop a tentative list of questions dealing specifically with interviewee's connection with Colegio. When conducting interview, verify file card information and then begin tentative question list. Tape recording and field notes will be made of each interview.

3. Transcribe each interview and make two copies. On one copy, highlight interview themes and special points of interest. Note any follow-up questions to be pursued.

4. Accumulate transcripts. Review accumulated transcripts, noting recurring themes. Categorize common themes, select project themes and assign color coding.

5. Review each transcript, highlighting on the second copy project themes with assigned color.

6. Develop argument and write narrative of each project theme.

Screening of Institutional and Public Records

1. Make a list of pertinent records. Identify and locate specific records, seek permission to review them.

    Complete a document record file for each record.

      Type of Record: Author/Source:

      Location: Date of Record:

      Record Synopsis:

      Themes:

      Can record be copied?   Yes   No

2. Color code record file card according to theme. If copy is available, highlight points of interest in corresponding color code.

3. Incorporate document information into project arguments and written narrative.

Secondary Sources

Make a list of secondary sources (newspaper and journal articles, etc.) Review articles, copy most useful and highlight themes in color code. Incorporate article information into project arguments and written narrative.

Interview Consent Form

Date:

CONSENT AGREEMENT TO PARTICIPATE

Before you formally agree to participate in this study, it is important that you be aware of and understand the following information. Please read the information below.

1. The purpose of this research is to investigate ethnic institutions of higher education. The researcher will focus on producing an institutional history of Colegio Cesar Chavez. This research will contribute to research focusing on Chicano educational history.

2. Your participation will consist of taking part as an interviewee. Interviews will be approximately one to one and one-half hours. The norm will be one interview per person unless a follow-up interview is necessary for clarification or extension of previous interview.

3. The interviews will be recorded, transcribed and excerpts integrated into the text of a research document.

4. The researcher has permission to: Use my name, position or status with Colegio, and quotes from the(se) interview(s) Use only my position or status with Colegio along with quotes from interview(s).

5. As a volunteer you may decline to participate at any point in the study.

The study described above has been explained to me. I understand and voluntarily consent to participate as an interviewee.

(Participant/Interviewee)

Carlos Maldonado—Researcher

Bibliography

BOOKS

Breneman, David W., and Finn, Chester E. Jr., ed. *An Uncertain Future*. Washington, D.C.: Brookings Institute, 1978.

Carnegie Foundation for the Advancement of Teaching. *A Classification of Institutions of Higher Education*, Princeton, N.J., 1987.

Carranza, Elihu. *Chicanismo: Philosophical Fragments*. Dubuque, Iowa: Kendall/Hunt Publishing Co., 1978.

Chicano Coordinating Council on Higher Education. *El Plan de Santa Barbara: A Chicano Plan for Higher Education*. Santa Barbara, Calif.: La Causa Publication, 1970.

Colegio Cesar Chavez Catalog. Mt. Angel, Ore.: Colegio Cesar Chavez, 1978.

Colegio Cesar Chavez Catalog. Mt. Angel, Ore.: Colegio Cesar Chavez, 1975.

Colegio Cesar Chavez Student Handbook. Mt. Angel, Oregon: Colegio Cesar Chavez, n.d.

Freire, Paulo. *Pedagogy of the Oppressed*. New York: The Seabury Press, 1970.

Gutierrez, Jose Angel. *The Making of a Militant: Lessons from Cristal*. Madison: The University of Wisconsin Press, 1998.

Hanford, George A. "Barriers to Higher Education Revisited" in *Equality Postponed: Continuing Barriers to Higher Education in the 1980s,* ed. Stephen H. Addphus. New York: College Entrance Examination Board, 1984.

Hernandez, Francisco Javier. *Schools for Mexicans: A Case Study of a Chicano School*. Stanford, Calif.: Stanford University, 1982.

Hill, Susan T. *The Traditionally-Black Institutions of Higher Education: 1860 to 1982*. Washington, D.C., National Center for Education Statistics, Department of Education: U.S. Government Printing Office, 1984.

Mayhew, Lewis B., ed. *Higher Education in the Revolutionary Decades*. Berkeley, Calif.: McCutchan Publishing Corp., 1967.

McKissack, Elena Aragón de. *A Case Study of Two High Schools: One Public, the Other Private and Chicanocentric*. Boulder: University of Colorado, Boulder, 1998.

Moreno, Jose F. ed. *The Elusive Quest For Equality: 150 Years of Chicana/Chicano Education*. Cambridge: Harvard Educational Review, 1999.

Muñoz, Carlos Jr. *Youth, Identity, Power: The Chicano Movement*. New York: Verso, 1989.

Nason, John. *Nature of Trusteeship: The Role and Responsibilities of College and University-Boards*. Washington, D.C.: Association of Governing Boards of Universities and Colleges, 1982.

Navarro, Armando. *The Cristal Experiment: A Chicano Struggle For Community Control*. Madison: The University of Wisconsin Press, 1998.

Oppelt, Norman T. *The Tribally Controlled Indian Colleges: The Beginnings of Self Determination In American Indian Education*. Tsaile, Ariz.: Navajo Community College Press, 1990.

The Politics of Mass Society. Cited by Abelardo Valdez, "Selective Determinants in Maintaining Social Movement Organizations: Three Case Studies from the Chicano Community." p. 30, n.p., n.d.

Ravitch, Diane. *The Troubled Crusade: American Education, 1945–1980*. New York: Basic Books, 1983.

Roman, Gilbert D. "Chicano Alternatives in Higher Education" in *Chicanos in Higher Education*, ed. Henry J. Casso and Gilbert D. Roman. Albuquerque: University of New Mexico Press, 1976.

Rudolph, Fredrick. *The American College and Universities*. New York: Knopf Inc., 1962.

Sanchez, Juan Jose. *A Study of Chicano Alternative Grade Schools in the Southwest: 1978–1980*. Boston: Harvard University, 1982.

Stein, Wayne J. *Tribally Controlled Colleges: Making Good Medicine*. New York: Peter Lang Publishing, 1992.

Union for Experimenting Colleges and Universities. *The University Without Walls: A First Report*. Yellow Springs, Ohio: Union for Experimenting Colleges and Universities, 1972.

The Uses of the University. Cited by Diane Ravitch, *The Troubled Crusade: American Education 1945–1980*, New York: Basic Books, 1983.

Valdez, Avelardo. "Selective Determinants in Maintaining Social Movement Organizations: Three Case Studies From the Chicano Community." n.p., n.d.

Vigil, Ernesto B. *The Crusade for Justice: Chicano Militancy and the Government's War on Dissent.* Madison: The University of Wisconsin Press, 1999.

JOURNALS

Crossland, F. E. "Learning to Cope with a Downward Slope." *Change* (July–August 1980), p. 18.

Estrada, Leobardo F.; Garcia, F. Chris; Macias, Reynaldo Flores; and Maldonado, Lionel. "Chicanos in the U.S.: A History of Exploitation and Resistance." *Daedalus*, no. 2 (Spring 1981), p. 122.

Kalvelage, Joan. "Cinco Exemplos." *Edcentric* (n. d.), p. 36.

Olivas, Michael A. "Indian, Chicano, and Puerto Rican Colleges: Status and Issues." *Bilingual Review*, no. 1 (1982), p. 36.

San Miguel, Guadalupe. "Status of the Historiography of Chicano Education: A Preliminary Analysis." History of Education Quarterly Winter 1986, p. 523–536.

St. John, Edward P.; and Byce, Charles. "The Changing Federal Role in Student Financial Aid." *New Directions for Higher Education*, no. 40 (1980), p. 30.

NEWSPAPERS

"Accreditation Goal for Struggling Colegio Cesar Chavez." *Oregonian*, 16 March 1981, p. 61.

"Ailing Colegio Endures Many Death Scenes." *Oregon Journal*, 12 October 1981, p. 7.

"Chavez Vows Fight for Colegio" *Oregonian*, 28 October 1977, p. Bi.

"Colegio Awaits Word as Eviction Nears." *Oregon Statesman*, 14 June 1977, p. A7.

"Colegio Backers Will Demonstrate." *Oregon Statesman*, 28 March 1975, sec. 4 p. 36.

"Colegio Desperately Tries to Stay Alive." *Oregon Journal*, 20 November 1976, p. 3.

"Colegio Officials are Optimistic After Meeting with HUD in D.C." *Oregon Statesman*, 14 May 1977, sec. 1, p. 1.

"Colegio Officials File Discrimination Charge." *Capital Journal*, 5 June 1974, sec. 1, p. 1.

"Colegio Officials to Confer in D.C. on Foreclosure." *Oregon Statesman*, 10 May 1975, sec. 1, p. 8.

"Colegio Ordered Off Mt. Angel Site." *Oregonian*, 3 September 1976, p. 1.

"Colegio Salutes First Graduating Class." *Oregonian*, 1 July 1977, sec. 3 p. All.

"Colegio Sit-in Planned to Protest Eviction Notice." *Capital Journal*, 26 March 1975, sec. 1, p. 1.

"Colegio Staff Believes Future Looks Bright." *Oregon Statesman*, 18 October 1975, sec. 2, p. 18.

"Colegio to HUD, Buy Your Own Set of Keys." *Oregon Statesman*, 14 January 1977, p. A2.

"Colegio Vows to Battle New HUD Eviction Order." *Oregon Statesman*, 3 March 1978, p. All.

"Colegio Wins Temporary Reprieve." *Oregon Statesman*, 8 July 1977, p. Cl.

"Colegio's Aims are Valid Despite Financial Plight." *Oregon Statesman*, 30 August 1976, p. Bl.

"College Named for Chavez." *Capital Journal*, 13 December 1973, sec. 2, p. 13.

"Evicted Colegio Demands HUD Practices be Probed." *Salem* (Ore.) *Oregon Journal*, 21 September 1977, p. 1.

"Festivities to Begin Tonight." *Oregon Statesman*, 12 December 1979, p. 16.

"Give Colegio to Chicanos, Measure Asks." *Oregon Statesman*, 7 May 1975, sec. 2, p. 23.

"HUD Considering Foreclosure on Mt. Angel College." *Silverton Appeal-Tribune*, 15 November 1973, p. 1.

"HUD Sells Campus to Chavez College for Quarter-Million." *Oregon Statesman*, 5 July 1978, p. Al.

"HUD Talks Tough on Colegio" *Capital Journal*, 1 April 1975, sec. 1, p. 1.

"Its Worst Crisis Over, Chicano College Forges Ahead." *Oregonian*, 17 February 1980, p. D15.

"MAC Board Votes to Remove Sister." *Silverton Appeal-Tribune*, 31 May 1973, p. 3.

"Major Gap Plagues Town, Gown at Mt. Angel." *Oregon Journal*, 5 December 1969, p. 6.

"Mondor Resigning MAC President." *Silverton Appeal-Tribune*, 18 October 1973, p. 1.

"Mt. Angel Takes New Name." *Oregon Journal*, 13 December 1973, p. 2.

"New Name Given College: Colegio Cesar Chavez." *Oregonian*, 13 December 1973, p. 47.

"Official Denies HUD Trying to Discourage Colegio." *Oregon Statesman*, 16 December 1976, p. A8.

"Response to Colegio's Suit Delayed for Legal Advice." *Oregonian*, 20 June 1977, p. B1.

"There is Room for Compromise in Colegio Cesar Chavez Case." *Statesman Journal-Capital Journal*, 2 October 1977, p. D3.

"75 March Through Portland Rain for Colegio Cesar Chavez." *Oregon Statesman*, 7 December 1976, p. C1.

GOVERNMENT DOCUMENTS

Brown v. Board of Education of Topeka, Kansas, 349 U.S. 483 (1954).

U.S. Department of Education. National Center for Education Statistics. *1997 Directory of Postsecondary Institutions*. Volume I, Degree-Granting Institutions, Project Officers, Samuel Barbett And Austin Lin. Washington, D.C.: U.S. Government Printing Office, 1998.

U.S. Department of Education, National Center for Education Statistics. *The Condition of Education 1998*, by John Wirt, Tom Snyder, Jennifer Sable, Susan P. Choy, Yupin Bae, Janis Stennett, Allison Gruner, and Marianne Perie. Washington, D.C.: U.S. Government Printing Office, 1998.

UNPUBLISHED MATERIAL

Candelaria, Dr. Cordelia. "Toward Securing Full Accreditation: Colegio Cesar Chavez Consultation with Dr. Cordelia Candelaria, Site Visit 1." 23 June, 1980.

Candelaria, Dr. Cordelia. "Toward Securing Full Accreditation: Colegio Cesar Chavez Consultation with Dr. Cordelia Candelaria. Site Visit II." 21 November 1980.

City of Mt. Angel. "Correspondence between the City of Mount Angel and Oregon Department of Transportation, Removal of Hi-way Directional Signs." 1982.

Colegio Cesar Chavez. "Annual Report to Northwest Association of Schools and Colleges." 1 March 1976.

Colegio Cesar Chavez. "Application and Proposal for Federal Support Under Title III, Basic Institutional Development Program." 26 April 1978.

Colegio Cesar Chavez. "Colegio Cesar Chavez Graduates, June 30, 1977." Appendix A of "Progress Report Submitted to Northwest Association of Schools and Colleges." Mt. Angel, Oregon, 14 April 1978.

Colegio Cesar Chavez (Mt. Angel, Oregon). Minutes of Meetings of the Board of Trustees, 1980–81.

Colegio Cesar Chavez. "National Demonstration Flyer." Mt. Angel: Colegio Cesar Chavez, n.d.

Colegio Cesar Chavez. "Press Release Concerning the Purchase of Campus." n.d.

Colegio Cesar Chavez. "Report of the Chair on the Consensus of the Board at Retreat: Regarding the Presidential Search." 29 October 1980.

Colegio Cesar Chavez. "Transcription of Tape Recording of Termination Hearing." 5 June 1980.

Colegio Cesar Chavez v. Northwest Association of Schools and Colleges. Doc. #85 Wheeling. (U.S. District Court), 37 (1977).

Colegio Cesar Chavez v. Northwest Association of Schools and Colleges. II Crist. (U.S. District Court), 383 (1977).

Colegio Cesar Chavez v. Northwest Association of Schools and Colleges. IV McCloskey. (U.S. District Court), 899 (1977).

Concerned Community for Colegio Cesar Chavez. "Agenda of Concerns." 26 March 1981.

Jellema, William W., and Hunter, William A., Consultants to the Department of Health, Education, and Welfare. "Report to the Director of Accreditation and Institutional Eligibility Staff: Department of Health, Education and Welfare; Office of Education, Bureau of Postsecondary Education Concerning Colegio Cesar Chavez." 30 April 1975.

National Hispanic University. "Institutional Introductory Literature." Oakland, California, n.d.

Northwest Association of Schools and Colleges. "Candidate for Accreditation: Biennial Evaluation." 11 May 1978.

Romero, Jose. "Chronological History of Colegio Cesar Chavez." Personal Files of Jose Romero, Salem, Oregon.

Staff of Colegio Cesar Chavez. "Staff Memo to Final Presidential Candidates." 1 October 1980.

INTERVIEWS

Aaberg, Robin. Ms. Aaberg's home, Hillsboro, Oregon. Interview, 7 April 1986.

DeGarmo, Peter. Mr. DeGarmo's home, Portland, Oregon. Interview, 3 April 1986.

Garcia, Jose. Oregon State Department of Education, Salem, Oregon. Interview, 9 April 1986.

Montez, Celedonio "Sonny." Inter-face Inc., Portland, Oregon. Interview, 18 April 1986.

Romero, Jose. Marion Educational Service District, Salem, Oregon. Interview, 14 April 1986.

Index

Printed in the United States
by Baker & Taylor Publisher Services